Beyond Hunger in Africa

CONVENTIONAL WISDOM
AND A VISION OF AFRICA IN 2057

Beyond Hunger in Africa

CONVENTIONAL WISDOM
AND A VISION OF AFRICA IN 2057

With a Foreword
by
Akin L. Mabogunje
Chairman of the Beyond Hunger Project

Editors:
CHINUA ACHEBE
GORAN HYDEN
ACHOLA PALA OKEYO
CHRISTOPHER MAGADZA

 Heinemann Kenya · Nairobi

 James Currey · London

 Heinemann · Portsmouth (N.H.)

Published by
Heinemann Kenya Limited
Brick Court, Mpaka Road/Woodvale Grove
P.O. Box 45314
Nairobi

ISBN 9966-46-818-6

in association with

James Currey
www.jamescurrey.com
is an imprint of Boydell & Brewer Ltd
PO Box 9, Woodbridge, Suffolk IP12 3DF, UK
and of Boydell & Brewer Inc.
668 Mt Hope Avenue, Rochester, NY 14620, USA
www.boydellandbrewer.com

ISBN978-0-85255-345-9

and

Heinemann Educational Books Inc.
361 Hanover Street, Portsmouth
New Hampshire 03801-3959

ISBN 978-0-435-08051-8

© The Beyond hunger Project 1990
First Published 1990

Transferred to digital printing

Typeset by
Type Design Limited
Kijabe Street, P.O. Box 8519
Nairobi

Contents

Preface vii
Foreword by Akin L. Mabogunje xi

PART 1: BY WAY OF INTRODUCTION 1
1 The Twin Challenge 3
2 Methodology of the Beyond Hunger Workshop 18

PART 2: THE CONVENTIONAL WISDOM: A SUMMARY 25
3 Projecting the Current Perspective 27

PART 3: AN ALTERNATIVE VISION: FOUR FUTURE HISTORIES 79
  Introduction 81
4 The Big Lift: A Journalist's Account 83
5 The Big Lift: A Scientist's Reflections 91
6 The Big Lift: Kericho Revisited 103
7 The Big Lift: A Report to the OAU 111
8 Conclusions: Levers of Change and Implications for Research and Policy 131

Appendix: List of Participants in the Beyond Hunger Project 137

Index 141

Preface

In the past twenty-five years, the image of Africa has shifted from great optimism to immense pessimism. In the minds of many, Africa is now a continent in crisis, a highly vulnerable region of the world. Famine, high population growth rates and declining agricultural production have to the external world rapidly become the most common symbols of African existence, replacing other historically entrenched stereotypes.

The persisting negative image of Africa as a continent in crisis, if unchallenged, may not only be misleading but may also cause articulate Africans to doubt their own self-determination and critical role as levers of change for a better future. In the absence of *credible alternative visions*, prevailing forecasts about Africa's future extrapolated from current trends and conventional analysis but leaving no scope for unanticipated events, could become self-fulfilling prophecies, frustrating the marshalling of the innovative thinking, creativity and energy needed for new directions of thought and action.

A number of Africans who represent a broad range of academic disciplines and institutions and who see a need to break the hold of present limited perceptions of the continent are beginning to make their voices heard around the region and in international forums concerning a possible direction for Africa in the twenty-first century. While they do not underestimate the legacies of the past and their consequent structural constraints as such, they are concerned about the need to restore confidence in the capacity of Africa to survive and indeed thrive in the future.

Africa cannot forever be haunted by its past. After all, many cataclysmic events of the past, like the Jewish Holocaust or the Hiroshima bombings of 1945, have not led to eternal pessimism among the Jews and the Japanese. It might even be said that these events have created a basis for overcoming inadequacies inherent in technology, economy or policy, so that they become levers of positive change.

Amidst today's difficulties, Africa needs new, magnetic images and aspirations for the future. This is a time that calls for creativity in working together across academic disciplines, policy institutions and political programmes in order to mobilize intellectual, managerial and financial resources toward a new Africa. This is a time that calls for greater self-criticism and reflection on the shortcomings of the past and the present. The Beyond Hunger Project represents an effort aimed at mobilizing continent-wide support for a new kind of imaging of Africa's future as a basis for formulating and implementing alternative development strategies.

What will Africa look like in the year 2057 — a century after Sudan and Ghana initiated the wave of political independence in sub-Saharan Africa? Usually nobody adopts such a long-term perspective. For governments, donor agencies and many others, including the media reporting on Africa, the future ends at the year 2000. Yet, in development terms a dozen years is nothing and a child born today will be below 70 years old in 2057.

Recognizing the need for a realistic time-frame for Africa's future development and for broadening of policy and research agenda beyond their current limits, three institutions — the Nairobi-based African Academy of Sciences, the Dakar-based Council for the Development of Economic and Social Research in Africa (CODESRIA), and the Alan Shawn Feinsten World Hunger Program, based at Brown University, USA — are currently sponsoring the research and development policy venture entitled the Beyond Hunger Project. The Project's initial activity was a workshop on Africa's future held at the Tea Hotel, Kericho, Kenya, on June 1-5, 1987. The proceedings of that workshop make up this volume.

Nineteen prominent African scholars drawn from ten different sub-Saharan countries and various academic backgrounds (see Appendix) came together at Kericho to consider the "conventional wisdom" about Africa's future and create through the use of a newly developed methodology alternative and surprise-rich scenarios for Africa. Participants were nominated by an Organizing Committee consisting of Professor Akin Mabogunje, Nigeria; Professor Thomas Odhiambo, Kenya; Dr Marie-Angelieque Savanne, Senegal; and Dr Goran Hyden, Sweden. Nominees were chosen for their documented commitment to and interest in Africa's future, for their scholarly contribution to the understanding and resolution of current problems, and for their readiness to think and articulate issues in an independent fashion.

The workshop was funded by grants from the Ford Foundation, the Royal Norwegian Ministry of Development Co-operation and the Swedish International Development Authority.

PREFACE

This volume differs from the typical academic book in at least two respects. The first is that it is a collective effort. No single participant has written a particular chapter or made a contribution that is more than anybody else's. Thus, no chapter carries an author's name. The book is being distributed in the name of the Project. A major reason for this approach is to emphasize the creativity that is inherent in collective or group efforts of this kind. It was the interaction among the different participants at the workshop that produced the contents of this volume. We wish to demonstrate, therefore, that human creativity can be mobilized through the use of methodologies that permit group interaction. On the basis of the experience at Kericho, we are ready to recommend it to others interested in developing alternative visions or strategies.

The second difference is that this volume does not look to the past, as does the typical academic text, but to the future. Academics groomed in the conventional epistemologies and methodologies, say of the social sciences, may find themselves ill at ease with the way we have gone about the exercise. We must emphasize, however, that the purpose of subject probability assessment and imaging—the two techniques used at the workshop to produce an alternative vision—is not to to provide answers but to raise new questions. By avoiding deductive analysis, typical of positivist approaches to the study of societies—whether in their liberal or Marxist trappings—we have wanted to erase the barriers to a better understanding of Africa's potential that such analysis poses. By opening the door to an alternative future scenario for Africa, we have attempted to focus attention on issues that otherwise would not be raised.

It is in the light of these considerations that this volume should be read. We hope that it will stimulate a debate among Africans and among others about what needs to be done today and tomorrow to achieve a sustainable development in the twenty-first century. We invite individual scholars and others particularly in Africa to contact us if they are interested in helping to move this effort forward.

On behalf of the Beyond Hunger Project,

Achola Pala Okeyo	*Christopher Magadza*	*Chinua Achebe*
Co-Editor	*Co-Editor*	*Co-Editor*
c/o ICIPE	*University Lake*	*Department of English*
P.O. Box 30772	*Kariba Research Station*	*University of Nigeria*
Nairobi, KENYA	*P.O. Box 48*	*Nsukka, NIGERIA*
	Kariba, ZIMBABWE	

Foreword

Over the ages, man has always been fascinated by the future. Its uncertainties and improbabilities have tantalised him to the point where he has been forced to seek various ways of prying open its tightly closed doors. Virtually every human society has its own category of soothsayers, diviners, seers, astrologers, stargazers and various others who claim they can see into the future. Even in modern times, such future merchants still thrive at the margin of the most developed industrial society. Science and literature have not been indifferent to this fascination. Writers of science fiction give their imagination a free rein to constitute possible landscapes and social-scapes of the future. Analytical scientific methods have also been used to project various futures from the present as the basis for determining policies and programmes which can affect these futures in preferred directions. These methods have indeed come to constitute the "conventional" wisdom of assaying the future.

Nonetheless, one of the most interesting realisations of recent times is the fact that when the present is thought of as the future of the past, its most outstanding characteristic is its closeness more to what would have passed as science fiction at a given vantage point in the past rather than to the product of such "conventional wisdom". What is clear therefore is that scientific methods to-date have not as yet given us an effective handle to prise open the surprisingly rich prospects of the future except perhaps in the very short-run. Beyond this, actual events in the future read stranger than present fiction.

The intriguing question, therefore, is: why do people want to know about their future? The simple answer is: because they wish to know how to react to their present circumstances, with what measure of care, courage, prudence and determination they should confront the on-rush of events. In other words, if they could only know the future, what must they try to do to get there?

All of these commonsensical ideas have informed new interests in studying the future. In this volume we are provided an almost revolutionary example of one of such new approaches applied, as it were, to getting a handle on the future of the African continent. Over the period which would make a hundred years from the time of the political independence of Ghana, that is the period 1957 to 2057, the African continent has already shown within three decades how easy it is to go from grace to grass. But what do the remaining seven decades hold in store for the continent? This volume, to my mind, does not claim to know the answer. But it has a healthy suspicion that it will not be what present conventional wisdom leads us to expect. By presenting us instead with a number of alternative scenario of possible "surprising" processes or paths leading to certain pre-determined end states, it has certainly excited the imagination and challenged our creative powers and energies to see whether Africans can make that future prospect come to life. The challenge is really whether through structured research, informed policy and dedicated policy implementation directed towards a perceivable and possible future goal, we in Africa may have created for ourselves a self-fulfilling future of our imagination and dream.

The future, indeed, may be uncertain. What is certain about it is that it will, as always, be rich in surprises. Through a series of well considered and articulated paths, this book presents us with the type of surprises which could lead to any one of possible futures for Africa.

Reading this book is a must not only for African scholars and scientists but more importantly for policy makers and political leaders. It gives a new twist to events and dispels the present pall of pessimism which currently envelopes the continent. It suggests that perhaps the present crisis is no more than a phase in the evolution of the continent. More importantly, it asserts that it is a phase out of which the continent may rise to higher achievements only if its leaders and its people dare to dream, to work imaginatively at their dreams and to strive to translate these dreams through research and action to concrete achievements.

African scholars and scientists, African leaders and policy makers, can we dare?

Akin L. Mabogunje
Chairman of the Beyond Hunger Project
Ibadan
1st December, 1989

Part 1
By Way of an Introduction

1

The Twin Challenge

The Challenge of Africa

Two decades ago, Africa's future was generally painted in bright colours. Having gained political independence, Africans and their many well-wishers in the international community assumed that the principal obstacle to progress had been removed. Independence was a prelude to victory. The primary challenge was to organize the political machinery for the multiple tasks of development. Whether the guiding ideology was "pragmatic" or "revolutionary", development was equal to modernization from above. If it was not the foreign expert who had the answers to Africa's problems, it was the African ideologue. Such was—on the political right or left—the conventional wisdom in the first decade after independence. One well-placed observer further argued that compared to the other Third World regions, Africa was the "easy" continent to develop[1]. It was free from the social misery that characterized Asia and Latin America. Nor did it have a single cultural or religious legacy that was likely to hold back modernization.

Today the story is different. The predominant perspective on Africa's future is gloomy. It is as one-sidedly pessimistic as the earlier one was optimistic. The pendulum has swung from one extreme to the other. In the last five years—particularly after the 1983/4 drought—there has been a growing convergence of opinion between African governments and international organizations that Africa is a special "emergency" case. The result has been the adoption of a "crisis" perspective on Africa which lies at the bottom of official statements issued both by African and international sources. To be sure, the available statistics indicate a grim picture: declining agricultural production, stagnating industrial production, deteriorating infrastructure, and falling living standards. These figures cannot be ignored. The question, however, is how far should they be allowed to determine our thinking about the future of Africa.

Perhaps the most tragic aspect of this situation is that the debate about Africa's future is dominated by the international community. Those who are farthest removed from the African realities—who do not feel the pinch or who need not take responsibility—are the pace-setters. In fact, even more than in the past, the prevailing notion is that Africa cannot move ahead without the aid of the international community. The current formula is the "compact", a mutual undertaking requiring commitment to long-term support by international donors in exchange for an African commitment to implement reforms and improve economic performance. Even well-intended efforts in this direction, such as the initiative taken by the Council of Foreign Relations in the United States in 1985/86[2] are essentially produced for an American audience by non-Africans, yet what its document says is expected to be "mainstream" in ideas not only in the West but also in Africa. The problem with this and other publications by official agencies on Africa is that they only tell part of the story. What these agencies write on Africa is more striking in what they do not say than in what they say. Reports by the World Bank, United Nations agencies and various other international organizations, including self-appointed watchdogs like the Worldwatch Institute, have become much more influential in African affairs than Africa's own mouthpieces, including the Organization of African Unity.

As the "crippled" region of the world, Africa is largely treated in a paternalistic fashion. This attitude towards the continent tends to be reinforced by the extent to which African governments see the future progress of their countries tied to the increased flow of external resources. While the predicament of many African governments today can be appreciated, it must also be admitted that it is to a very large extent self-inflicted. In the name of "quick" progress, these governments have turned to external resources rather than explore and encourage the full potential of domestic resources, whether natural or human. This, in turn, has put a premium on inter-governmental resource transfers and on the state as the monopolistic agency of change. While African governments today, partly by their own volition, partly under pressure from the International Monetary Fund, are reviewing and revising their past policies, there is still an understandable inclination in such circles to view increased flows of outside resources as a less costly option than initiating economic and political reforms that would permit a more effective utilization of Africa's own resource potential.

In brief, Africa today suffers in particular because of the following

three shortcomings:
- The image of Africa is one-sided
- Africa's own voice is ignored
- Africa's domestic capacity is neglected.

"Beyond Hunger"—a Response

The "Beyond Hunger: Africa's Future 1957-2057" Project has been started in order to address these shortcomings. By adopting a centennial time-perspective, the Project hopes to bring to bear on the debate about Africa issues that are intentionally or unintentionally concealed by the conventional "crisis" perspective. It wants to demonstrate that Africa is much more than famine and debt and that it possesses both a will and a capacity to reverse the current trend on its own. To do so, at least two preconditions have to be fulfilled. The first is the need to create new, magnetic images of the future that can shape policy, action and research. The second is the need for a more pluralist policy environment. At independence, the creation of future scenarios was the exclusive monopoly of Africa's political leadership. The visionaries were also the heads of state. In today's difficult situation, where mobilization of domestic resources is slowly emerging as the new emphasis, the task of thinking about the future has to be shared by as many Africans as possible. Africa's intellectuals have a special responsibility to participate in this task. That is why, at least at this initial phase of the Project, it addresses itself to the intellectual community and its concerns about the present shortcomings of the continent.

The name of this project could equally well have been "Beyond Underdevelopment", but we deliberately chose "Beyond Hunger" for two reasons. The first is that "hunger" is the stigma most strongly attached to Africa today. It is both one-sided and conjectural and for this reason this Project looks beyond it. Secondly, to the extent that hunger is a reality in Africa, it is a target within reach and more specific than the diffuse concept of "underdevelopment". This does not mean that those involved in this Project ignore the issues of underdevelopment, notably the structural dimensions of Africa's present predicament; they are indeed very much part of the backdrop against which this Project is being pursued.

Yet we do not want to be caught in the pessimism or despair that flow from too rigid an adherence to structuralist theories. Africa cannot for ever continue to be haunted by its past. Nor do we want to adopt the false optimism associated with the "structural adjustment" policies now pursued by African governments in collaboration with the international finance institutions. While some elements contained in these efforts clearly are necessary steps in the right direction, the individualist and utilitarian ideals underlying these approaches are overly simple. They simply do not relate to much of the complex social reality in Africa.

The assumption underlying the Beyond Hunger Project is, as Marx once put it, that "men (or better, human beings) make history, but not in circumstances of their own choosing". In that sense, there are limits to what humans can undertake at any one time, though the extent of change possible would obviously vary depending on whether, for example, the circumstances are "day-to-day" or extraordinary. What is emphasized here is the potential power of the capacity of humankind to reflect on events and thus the role that culture plays as a catalyst for change. People do not discover their full potential unless encouraged and enabled to develop a sense of who they are, what their worth is, and how these sentiments can be translated into meaningful social interaction. This is a universal observation but it has particular relevance to Africa, a continent whose culture has for centuries been denigrated. The self-esteem and self-confidence that turn human beings into agents of change will only come about as a result of greater respect for and recognition of the role culture plays in society.

The project argues that a prerequisite for the better utilization of Africa's material or natural resources (and hence a reversal of the current downward trend) is the continent's discovery of itself. This, in turn, requires a much greater concern with the need for public debates about fundamental philosophical, cultural and political issues. Denying Africans the opportunity or right to such debates is as much part of the underdevelopment syndrome as is the continent's economic dependence on the Western world.

By opening the door to the future in a way that no other comparable efforts are doing, this project intends to facilitate the broadening of the policy debate by going beyond the most urgent and sensitive issues. It does not ignore them but places them in a time-perspective that permits both increased detachment and a greater appreciation of alternatives.

There may be those in Africa who believe that what we need today is more effective action rather than more research and more debate about issues. While this attitude of mind is understandable given the critical nature of the situation in many parts of the continent, "Beyond Hunger" does not agree with that position. Africa has no ready-made path forward. Due respect should be paid to the efforts by African political leaders to identify an African development strategy—the Lagos Plan of Action—but it would be wrong to assume that a single-minded implementation of that plan is the sole path forward. The Lagos Plan of Action rightly emphasizes "African" but to that must be added "multiple" and "pluralist", i.e. the assumption that there are many approaches and that they have to be assessed and carried out in a competitive and open policy environment.

This Project emphasizes also the need to go beyond the notion that all research as a public activity has to prove its worth by being relevant to a given society's needs and problems, "applied" research becomes meaningful only in a context which is effectively backed up by more "basic" research programmes. Given the absence of an indigenous research tradition in Africa, it is understandable that theories and concepts have been borrowed from other settings. The history of applied research in Africa, therefore, has been one of trial and error, using theories and concepts derived from non-African experiments and settings to decide what questions to pose, what form trials should take, and what kind of results to interpret. As African universities and other research institutions have become increasingly starved of public financial support, this trend has grown worse. The principal impetus for the growth of new knowledge and modification of subsequent efforts in Africa has been the detection of shortcomings or errors associated with imported theories and concepts. It has been a matter of discarding old theories rather than discovering new ones. Furthermore, the new knowledge thus created has been narrow and specialized. No attempts have been made to synthesize it with a view to assessing what it means for the future of Africa. In this situation it is not surprising that many development experiments have proved very costly to Africa.

Thus, Africa today needs both new questions and smaller errors. This Project is primarily concerned with the former, the assumption being that they are a prerequisite for adequately tackling the latter. There is sufficient scientific competence available in Africa today for new knowledge to be increasingly generated from within, as it were, through the realignment of research agenda away from the "short-term" and "applied" towards the longer term and more basic questions affecting the continent's future.

A first step in this direction is to examine critically the conventional wisdom as expressed in dominant policy documents related to Africa's present and future. This is the subject of chapter 3 in this volume, which presents both a summary statement of what current perspectives on Africa's future contain with regard to key variables such as population, agriculture, energy, economy, technology and human resources, and a critique of the assumptions and the data on which the perspectives are based.

The second step in realignment is the development of alternative future scenarios for Africa that challenge the "surprise-free" projections of the current perspectives. How "surprise-rich" scenarios can be generated is the subject of chapter 2. By spelling out the methodology used in this Project it sets the stage for the four "future histories" developed by participants in this Project and presented in chapters 4-7.

At this point suffice it to say that the image of a future Africa is treated here both as an object of research and as a statement of the problem. The image of the future is treated as a research problem precisely because the current perspectives on Africa are so closely tied up with acute problems and emergencies. That is why this Project calls on African intellectuals to engage in research that goes beyond the narrow horizons of the applied and policy-oriented studies that currently constitute the principal guides for thinking about Africa, present or future. The image of the future can also play an important role as a conceptual tool, adding to the diagnostic powers of science. The anticipatory image of the future is tested in the Project for its value in helping to write alternative future histories for Africa. Chapter 8 provides an assessment of this role and discusses the broader policy and research implications of the alternative "end state" used in formulating the future histories presented in chapters 4-7.

The Challenge of the Future

To place the Beyond Hunger Project in a comparative intellectual perspective, it may be helpful to see how its treatment of the future relates to the way others have responded to the challenge of the future. Every great thinker who has concerned himself with the historical process has speculated about the meaning of time and its flow in history. Hegel, Marx, Spengler, Sorokin and Toynbee—to name but a few—predict the future but ignore its dynamic interaction with the past and the present. By recognizing the interaction between completed and noncompleted time, this Project goes beyond the interpretation of history merely as mechanically patterned fluctuations. Thus, "development" is being viewed here as a push-pull process in which society is at once pulled forward by its own magnetic images of an idealized future and pushed from behind by its realized past. Poised on the dividing line between past and future is humankind, the unique bearer and transformer of cultural and material conditions.

Temporal images of the world have been variously projected into the distant future or into the past. The latter represent romantic idealizations of that past: the Biblical paradise, the golden age of Hesiod, or the Renaissance image of antiquity. Similarly, a good deal of contemporary African political thought has idealized the pre-colonial past. These dreams of the past operate on the future, though indirectly. As such, they engage people and provide the impetus for concerted social action in a way that proves very difficult in those situations where no temporal image—whether of the future or the past—is presented. Thus, while the past has often been used to rekindle the spirit of people, it is the future in particular that has attracted humanity's dreams, hopes, and fears. The future rather than the past is seen as holding the key to the riddle of human existence.

The domain of the future is without boundaries. It is only by drawing boundaries in the realm of thought, however, that people can produce a problem that can be grasped and worked with. Consequently, it is only by redrawing the boundaries of the unknown that they can increase their knowledge. In the act of searching out the future, as Polak reminds us[3], people cease to be merely actors, responding to the immediate, and transform themselves into planners, who take account of the consequences of action. The instincts of preservation and reproduction demand it. All economic activity is an answer to this challenge: the African nomad and the Western industrial magnate alike are answering the call of the unborn tomorrow. There is no difference in their existential rationality.

Once aware of a future, humanity has been increasingly concerned with knowing what the future will bring. The impulse to propitiate the powers of the future in order to avoid catastrophe and procure blessings may well have been part of the drive for knowledge from its early beginnings. Both magic and religion probably arose (at least in part) out of this twin drive for certainty and control. For many centuries humankind struggled to obtain a reliable reading of signs and omens, both in the heavens and in the world around. It seems likely that dependence on the direct inspiration of gifted specialists, whether priest or prophet, came later. As people elaborated their technology and embarked on the adventures of agriculture, navigation and their first large-scale engineering projects such as pyramids and waterworks, the need to predict and control the future became of still more practical urgency. The beginnings of science grew out of this urgency; astrology, and its more sober offspring, astronomy, alike served this need to know the future from a very early point onwards in history.

In the systemic study of the future we are compelled to exclude one of the most important sources of all knowledge: human experience. We can experience what has been, but not what is to be. We can experience what happened to those images and anticipated futures which now belong to the past. However, as soon as we want to change from *ex post* to *ex ante* knowledge, we have to tap supplementary sources. Only with the help of reason can the experience of the known provide a basis for useful extension into the unknown. Science has already take a long stride in the direction of predictions of the future by using models based on assumptions of specific periodicities and trends. Concepts of determinism, so prevalent in earlier philosophies, have given way to concepts of probability. At the same time, specialization in science has led to an examination of more and more minute segments of reality, moving further and further away from total patterns of any kind. Today's conventional forecast is highly segmented and totally "surprise-free", i.e. void of any reference to the probability of specific events or unexpected changes altering the predictions.

It would be wrong to assume, however, that science alone provides us with the means to explore the future. Non-rational tools have contributed—and continue to contribute—to thinking about the future. Faith has been the most important factor, with its ample tool-chest containing all the instruments of sacred knowledge. Next comes philosophical thought, meditation, and speculation. Last comes the realm of emotion, particularly those aspects concerned with hope, longing, and expectation. Intuition and ecstasy belong here, and most of all the power of the free creative imagination, which is indispensable to all thinking about the unknown. Thinking about the future, therefore, requires faith and vision, mixed with philosophical detachment, a rich emotional life and creative fantasy, as well as the rigorous and orderly tools of science.

In thinking rigorously but creatively about the future, one moves along a fine line between science fiction and futures science. Science fiction images of the future are, at their best, creative and imaginative. But they often involve such enormous changes from current perspectives that they require the creation of wholly fictional peoples, places, technologies, and times that bear little resemblance to what is currently known and anticipated. In contrast, most futures science employs the extrapolation of the currently known and anticipated in its most probable form to create 'surprise-free' futures. These unimaginative extensions of the status quo appear as unlikely as the improbable, but much more imaginative, creations of science fiction.

In developing new perspectives on Africa's future, the Beyond Hunger Project seeks to transcend what Brooks[4] calls an "evolutionary paradigm": the gradual, incremental unfolding of the world system in a manner that can be described by surprise-free models, with parameters derived from a combination of time-series and cross-sectional analyses of the existing system. This has been true of econometric models, of energy models, and of models of the global environment[5]. The evolutionary approach has its uses, particularly in elucidating long-term trends in broad scale patterns. But, for instance, as C. S. Holling has convincingly argued, experience shows that significant change can also occur in abrupt, discontinuous bursts. If there is no framework of expectation of discontinuity, then abrupt changes are perceived as surprises— as crises or opportunities[6]. Surprise-free forecasts are therefore necessary but insufficient tools for efforts to understand the problems and potential of the future. By leaving out the external shocks, non-linear responses and discontinuous behaviour so typical of both social and natural systems, surprise-free analysis leaves us unprepared to interpret a host of not otherwise improbable eventualities. By leaving out the social learning called into play by the resulting crises and opportunities, it also reduces the challenge of designing adaptive management strategies to a mindless, repetitive implementation of past mistakes.

To provide some sense of what is meant by surprise and discontinuity it may be helpful to list the kind of events that often arise in the interactions between technology, institutions, and development. Following Brooks'[7], we include the following:
- unexpected discrete events such as the oil shocks of 1973 and 1979, the Chernobyl reactor incident, political coups or revolutions, major natural catastrophes, accidental wars;
- discontinuities in long term trends, such as the acceleration of African food imports between 1974 and 1985, the onset of running inflation in the 1980s, and the growing debt burden of African countries; and
- the sudden emergence of new forms of social consciousness such as the need to plant trees or to stem the frequent violations of civil and human rights in many African countries.

These and other relevant examples are indicative of surprise in that they do not follow from conventional extrapolations or projections based on current thinking and trends.

The problem is not that analysts have been unaware of the shortcomings of surprise-free thinking, but rather that they lack usable methodologies to deal with discontinuities and random events. The multiplicity of conceivable surprises is so large and heterogenous that the analyst despairs of deciding where to begin, and instead proceeds in the hope that, in the longer sweep of history, surprises and discontinuities will average out, leaving smoother long-term trends as a basis for reasonable approximations to the future.

But real history turns out to be far from an 'averaging out'. The distinguished historian, William H. McNeill concluded his remarks at a symposium on 'Resources for an Uncertain Future' as follows:

> I believe historians' preoccupation with catastrophe might be useful to economists, if they care to listen. Extreme cases, breakdowns, abrupt interruptions of established market relations—these are not staples of economic theory, and are, I believe, usually dismissed by statistically minded analysts of the norm and its fluctuations. But human societies are a species of equilibrium, and equilibria are liable to catastrophe when, under special limiting conditions, small inputs may produce very large, often unforeseen, and frequently irreversible outputs. I believe there is a branch of

mathematics that deals with catastrophe—sudden changes in process; I must say that I, as an historian contemplating the richly catastrophic career of humanity across the centuries, venture to recommend to economists more attention and consideration of such models — at least when trying to contemplate the deeper and long-range future[8].

A central challenge to this Project is to see how far it can go in developing the concepts and methods necessary to move beyond surprise-free analyses to a more realistic treatment of the discontinuities that occur. The "catastrophe" theories and their relatives referred to by McNeill have played an important role in providing an alternative paradigm to surprise-free analysis. But to move beyond the empty generalities and vague analogies which have so far inflated the "catastrophe" literature, it will be necessary to assemble a family of specific techniques and explanatory models, and maybe go as far as to develop theories of surprise. The way Project participants embarked upon the task of developing alternative future scenarios and the issues associated therewith are further discussed in chapter 2.

Who are Involved?

It should be clear by now that it is the twin challenge of Africa and the future – one substantive, the other methodological – that provides the impetus for this Project. A growing number of Africans are genuinely concerned that famine has rapidly become the most common symbol of African life to the rest of the world, replacing other historically entrenched stereotypes. They are aware that the current crisis image of Africa, if unchallenged, may be misleading in many respects. The data base on which it rests is weak and unreliable; time horizons for evaluating trends on the continent are short; methodology is overly simple; and analysis is most distant (done mainly by "experts" based in international organizations outside Africa). But most important, in the absence of credible alternative visions, they believe, prevailing forecasts about Africa's future, extrapolated from current trends with no scope for unanticipated events, could become self-fulfilling prophecies, frustrating the marshalling of African creativity and energy for needed new directions.

The growing number of these concerned Africans, who see the need for breaking the hold of conventional perceptions about the continent, represent a broad range of institutions and professional backgrounds. The Beyond Hunger Project, which attempts to combine research and development policy issues in new ways, is unique in that it brings together intellectuals in a bold interdisciplinary venture. Natural and social scientists are having to come to terms with each other. Engineers are being asked to take novelists seriously. Medical doctors are having to come to terms with the wisdom of cultural anthropologists. Such accommodations do not come easily but provide the inherent challenge of the Project.

The initial effort of this Project—the workshop on "Beyond Hunger, Africa's future, 1957-2057" at Kericho, Kenya, the proceedings of which form the basis for this volume—was by invitation only. Participants in the workshop, however, resolved to constitute themselves into a network of concerned individuals. Other Africans who share this concern, whether they are based in universities, governments or non-governmental organizations, are being invited to join. (Those who are interested can write to the Project secretariat at the addresses listed in pp. 137-139.) A limited number of non-Africans who share the concern expressed above may be allowed to join the network, but it is important that this venture remain primarily African if it is to project an *African* perspective on the future of the continent.

The Project organizers are aware that this is by no means the only effort in the past ten years devoted to Africa's future. Important to mention here are the UNITAR/CODESRIA Conference on "Africa and the Future" (Dakar, 1977), the Monrovia Symposium on "Future Development Prospects in Africa" (Monrovia, 1978), and an OAU Seminar on "Alternative Patterns of Development and Life Styles for the Africa Region" (Addis Ababa, 1978). These essentially non-official consultations provided a constituency and framework for the major landmark in the continent's ideological volte face in the past few years: the April 1980 Economic Summit in Lagos that produced the Lagos Plan of Action. Of significance to this Project has also been the prospective study of Africa's development 1983-2008, published by the United Nations Economic Commission for Africa in conjunction with its twenty-fifth anniversary[9]. This Project also acknowledges the contributions made by the "Panel of Wise Men", a group of African scholars who met under the auspices of the United Nations University in 1984-5, the "Africa Year 2000" project, directed by Professor Samir Amin, also with UNU and UNITAR sponsorships; and we acknowledge work by scholars concerned with alternative futures for Africa, notably a series of publications edited or written by Timothy Shaw[10].

For those who are wondering about the methodological origin of this Project, it is important to mention that the basic elements used here are not new in themselves. Extrapolation from the present—used to develop the "surprise-free' scenario; subjective probability assessment —employed to identify alternative "end-states"; and imaging—applied with a view to conceiving credible, coherent and consistent pathways to the future end-points, have all been employed in varying degrees over the last few decades. The only other time, however, they have been used together as in this Project was at a workshop on the future of the biosphere, organized in Sweden in January 1986 by the Swedish Council for Planning and Co-ordination of Research in conjunction with the International Institute of Advanced Systems Analysis (IIASA)[11]. The relative success of that workshop, at which Professors Akin Mabogunje and Goran Hyden — chairman and secretary respectively of the organizing committee of this Project — were in attendance, was an inspiration for trying out its methodology in a modified fashion in relation to Africa's future.

The Project considers itself privileged to enjoy the sponsorship of three highly respected institutions: the African Academy of Sciences (AAS), the Council for Development of Economic and Social Research in Africa (CODESRIA), and the Alan Shawn Feinsten World Hunger Program (WHP). AAS was founded in 1985 under the auspices of the Third World Academy of Sciences, based at Trieste, Italy. The Academy's principal role is to develop Africa's own manpower and know-how and sensitize governments to the realization that no country can ever develop with borrowed skills and resources. More specifically, the Academy stimulates, designs and co-ordinates regional inter-disciplinary scientific research, promotes science education programmes, nurtures the growth of young scientists, and undertakes the publication of scientific progress in various media. It draws its membership from all over the continent. It has its headquarters in Nairobi, Kenya.

CODESRIA originated in 1973 as a forum for directors of development research institutes in Africa. In the later 1970s its mandate was expanded to include the development of social science research on the continent. It is currently the sole inter-African agency with such a mandate. It initiates and co-ordinates regional multi-disciplinary research projects on pertinent topics, awards research grants to promising young scholars, and promotes interaction among African social scientists through seminars and publications, including its own journal, *African Development*. Its headquarters is in Dakar, Senegal.

Started in 1986, the WHP, based at Brown University, Providence, RI, USA addresses two principal questions: (1) Why does hunger persist in a world of plenty? (2) How can hunger be eliminated in the foreseeable future? Using hunger as the cutting edge of its work rather than "food production", "nutrition" or any other such more narrow variable, the WHP initiates and co-ordinates multi-disciplinary research on such topics as the prospect for sustainable agriculture in the world and the possible outcomes of the "green gene revolution". Special importance is attached to a long-term perspective, both backwards and forwards, in studying hunger issues.

The first phase of this Project has received funding from three different sources: the Ford Foundation — $25,000; the Norwegian Ministry of Development Co-operation — $25,000; and the Swedish International Development Authority — $25,000.

To summarize this section; the Beyond Hunger Project complements earlier studies of the future of Africa in its attempt to enlarge and enhance the strength of the constituency of African scholars concerned about Africa's present and future. It goes beyond these earlier efforts by adopting a longer (and perhaps more realistic) time-perspective and by developing a new methodology for creating "surprise-rich" future scenarios. It must be emphasized, however, that the future histories contained in this volume should be read neither as forecasts nor as predictions. They constitute a vision of what is probable and possible. Thus, this volume is but the first step of the Project's work. By opening the door to the future, it has merely created a prologue to further interdisciplinary studies that will highlight the issues raised in the future histories. Yet in doing so, this Project is moving the research frontiers forward and thus, hopefully, making a contribution towards a more constructive debate about the continent's future.

NOTES

1. Guy Hunter, *Modernizing Peasant Societies*, London, Oxford University Press, 1969.
2. Overseas Development Council and Council on Foreign Relations, *Compact for African Development: Report of the Committee on African Development Strategies*, Washington D.C., 1986.

THE TWIN CHALLENGE 17

3. Fred Polak, *The Image of the Future*, Amsterdam, Elsevier Scientific Publishing Co., 1973.
4. Harvey Brooks, "The Typology of Surprises in Technology Institutions and Development" in W.C. Clark and R.E. Munn (eds), *Sustainable Development of the Biosphere*, Cambridge, Cambridge University Press, 1986.
5. See, e.g. Council on Environmental Quality, *Global 2000 Report to the President*, Washington DC, Government Printing Office, 1980; Office of Technology Assessment, *Global Models, World Future and Publishing Policy: a Critique*, Washington DC, Office of Technology Assessment, 1982; and M.L. Greenberger et al., *Caught Unawares: The Energy Decade Retrospect*, Cambridge, Mass., Ballinger, 1983.
6. C.S. Holling, "Resilience of Ecosystems: Local Surprise and Global Change" in W.C. Clark and R.E. Munn, *op. cit*, 1986.
7. Brooks, op. cit., p.6.
8. William H. McNeill, "Coping with an Uncertain Future — Historical Perspective" in C. Hitch (ed.), *Resources for an Uncertain Future*, Baltimore, Johns Hopkins University Press, 1979.
9. UN Economic Commission for Africa, ECA and Africa's Development 1983-2008, Addis Ababa, Economic Commission for Africa, 1983.
10. See Timothy M. Shaw (ed.), *Alternative Futures for Africa*, Boulder, Colorado, Westview Press, 1982; T.M. Shaw, "Debates about Africa's Future: The Brant, World Bank, and Lagos Plan Blueprints", *Third World Quarterly*, Vol. 5, No. 2 (April) 1983; and, T.M. Shaw and O. Aluko, (eds), *Africa Projected: From Recession to Renaissance by the Year 2000?*, New York, St Martin's Press, 1985.
11. Swedish Council for Planning and Coordinating Research, *Surprising Futures: Notes from an International Workshop on Long-term World Development*, Stockholm, Swedish Council for Planning and Cordinating Research, 1987.

2

Methodology of The Beyond Hunger Workshop

As indicated in chapter 1, participants in the Kericho workshop used a combination of different methodologies: (1) extrapolation from the present; (2) subjective probability assessment and perception; and (3) imaging. Although all three have been in existence for a long time, they have been used together only in the past few years.

Participants were first asked to consider a current perspective scenario of development in sub-Saharan Africa until the middle of the twenty-first century. This paper, which is reprinted here somewhat abbreviated as chapter 3, was sent to participants in advance, giving them a chance to consider prior to the meeting what the "conventional wisdom" about Africa's development over the next seventy years is. Derived from an analysis of approximately a hundred international documents projecting future trends in Africa (and the world) with regard to conventional indicators such as population growth, gross domestic product capabilities and social development, it constitutes a unique compilation of current perspectives about the continent. Nowhere else can a more comprehensive summary of the future projections for Africa be found.

The future scenario of Africa that emerges in the "conventional wisdom" perspective is surprise-free in that it does not attempt to encompass specific events, unexpected changes, or other surprises that could significantly alter long-term trends. As chapter 3 indicates, it differs from the Malthusian "persistent-trends" scenarios put forward by, for example, the Economic Commission for Africa or the Food and Agriculture Organization of the United Nations, in that it reflects conventional expectations of the reversal of recent discouraging trends in population growth, food production, economic performance, and other areas.

It is clear that surprise-free development over the next seventy years is not very likely. Few periods in history have not had their share of surprises. Nevertheless, the potential for surprise should not deter careful examination of and planning for the future. Indeed, according to World Bank demographic projections, of the 180 million children in Africa under

METHODOLOGY OF THE BEYOND HUNGER WORKSHOP   19

age 10 in 1985, roughly three-fifths are likely to survive to the age of 70 or more by 2055. In other words, at least one-fifth of Africa's current population may witness *all* that occurs during the next seventy years. The year 2057 will be of concern not only to members of future generations, but also to many of those alive today.

The current perspective scenario in chapter 3, then, provides the starting point for developing alternative scenarios of the future and for asking questions about how long present trends might persist, how they might be modified by ongoing or future choices, and how well they portray the future of Africa.

A three-stage trajectory is generally employed by international organizations in projecting the current perspective for Africa to 2057. The time of *euphoria* begins in 1957 and ends around 1980; the time of *trouble* continues to the end of the century; and the time of *renewal* extends to 2057. For many variables, each time implies a different growth rate. For instance, economic growth per capita is assumed to be 2.4 per cent per year for 1950-80, 1 per cent for 1980-2000, and 2.5 per cent for 2000-2057. Although the year 2000 appears to be a relatively early turning-point for some of the current discouraging trends, it is certainly a key reference point in the conventional wisdom about the future. Delaying the onset of the time of renewal to 2010 does not change the scenario for 2057 significantly, provided the same assumptions about the key indicators are accepted.

The first day of the workshop was devoted to reflecting on the conventional wisdom about Africa's future. In different degrees, participants had three principal reactions to the document. The first was that it was not optimistic enough. The assumption that Africa's growth rate in the twenty-first century would be only the same as between 1950-80 was questioned by many who suggested that if Africa can only get its economic and political house in order, the prospect for higher growth rates is clearly within the realm of possibility. The discussion that ensued did not overlook the fact that things might get worse before they get better, but even so, participants were generally agreed that the assumptions in the conventional wisdom scenario were too conservative.

A second reaction was that this scenario overlooked cultural variables and as such left without consideration the human element in the creation of history. Some participants took what would be tantamount to a "materialist" position and found themselves in agreement, if not with the substantive conclusions, at least the choice of indicators used in the conventional wisdom scenario. This division between "culturalists" and "materialists" recurred several times during the workshop.

The third reaction was that the current perspective on Africa's future is largely the product of non-African institutions and, as such, by people who have little sense of the realities in which the statistical data are being collected and analyzed. Underlying many comments, therefore, was an understandable aversion to the fact that the image of Africa is being created by non-Africans. It is important to point out, however, that in spite of this observation, at no time did participants diverge from the idea that the "blame" for Africa's current woes lies as much with the governments of the continent as it does with external factors. In fact, perhaps the most important note about the way the workshop operated is that every participant was ready to take a self-critical view of the present. Never was there any real push to lay the blame on the external environment only. In this respect the intellectual climate at the workshop was very different from what it would have been, had it been held ten years previously in the hey-day of the "dependency theory" approach.

In constructing alternative future scenarios, workshop participants used a combination of subjective probability assessment and imaging. The first of these two methodologies was used to elicit "surprising" or alternative endpoints for Africa in the year 2057. The second day of the meeting was devoted to brain-storming about these alternative "endpoints". The main point of this exercise was to encourage participants to think about a scenario that would surprise them. Working in four groups of five persons each, the participants produced two separate scenarios. The first was labelled the "Big Lift", based on the assumption that after another twenty to thirty years of turbulence and "reckoning", Africa would "take off". The second was called the "Big Rift", after participants had suggested that a very probable scenario for the mid-twenty-first century was an increasing differentiation among African states.

The original idea was that the four groups would continue their work by producing one future history for each of the two scenarios: the "Big Lift" and the "Big Rift". In the end, however, participants had time to produce a future history only for the first of those two. Two full days were spent in composing these histories and with only one day left, there was no time for the second end-point.

METHODOLOGY OF THE BEYOND HUNGER WORKSHOP

In composing the future history of the "Big Lift", participants used the technique of imaging. It proved demanding because all four groups were expected to come up with credible, coherent and consistent pathways to an alternative future. The "conventional wisdom" scenario was used in the group discussions to provide a sense of what statistics might or might not allow. Constant checks were being made by the groups' "number-crunchers" to ensure that the anticipated pathways did not take on the quality of science fiction or mere wishful thinking. As these future histories, reproduced here as chapters 4-7, indicate, a lot of intellectual creativity went into this particular part of the workshop. When finally emerging from this two-day, intensive exercise, everybody agreed that it had been great fun and had enabled them to think about Africa afresh. The future histories were all produced under different guises: as a speech by the Secretary General of the Organization of African Unity to the United Nations General Assembly, as lectures at African universities, and as a journalist's account of the centennial anniversary of Ghana's independence. We hope that some of the creative dimensions of the methodology used in this Project really shine through in the four chapters containing these future histories.

In evaluating the methodology used in the workshop, it should be said that it created its definite tensions among participants, particularly in the first two days. It is hard to know how much these tensions should be attributed to the facts that many participants were new to each other and they represented different academic disciplines and approaches. All the same, the newness of the methodology and the need to be a "team player" in a context where there were a number of uncertainties clearly also contributed to the initial tensions.

By allowing a longer time horizon than usual, however, this methodology also enabled participants of varying backgrounds to work effectively together without getting bogged down in epistemological differences. Thus, once the initial hesitation had been overcome, the exercise went very well. To be sure, divergences on many issues remained among partipants but it was encouraging to see how productively physicists, geographers, climatologists, economists, political scientists, anthropologists and novelists were able to work together in the interest of Africa's future.

While the seventy-year time horizon adopted in the Project at first appeared quite long—and indeed is much longer than that employed in current perspectives — participants soon realized that seventy years constitute a relatively short period in human history. The subjective probability assessment technique encouraged participants to recognize the importance of the human force in history. Man can make a difference, but he must also accept than not all events are equally probable. Much of the discussion in the groups was devoted to trying to assess which events that man sets in motion are likely to be particularly significant in the long run. Workshop participants identified a broad range of factors that tend to be ignored in current perspectives, for example, spontaneous innovations and productive activities taking place outside the formal sector, technological growth, political changes and climatic shifts. All of these can bring about surprising developments in Africa in the next seventy years, as is further discussed also in chapter 8.

At first glance, the alternative future scenarios produced by the workshop may appear overly optimistic, but that is a mistaken impression. In comparison with the "conventional wisdom" scenario, these alternatives assume a longer period of crisis, reckoning and awakening. At the same time, it adopts a more optimistic assumption about Africa's performance after year 2015. Contrary to the conventional wisdom which assumes a unilinear trend, the alternative future histories incorporate a dialectic movement, i.e. the notion that crisis and decline spur change and improvement.

Perhaps the most important outcome of the workshop was the growing awareness among participants that they represented a new movement that could have a bearing on where Africa is going in the next seventy years. There was a deliberate effort to contrast the thoughts, approaches and methodologies adopted in the workshop with those associated with the "conventional wisdom". There was a distinct sense that as Africans continue to think about the future of their continent, they must be bold enough to break out of the conventional wisdom and adopt approaches that make sense to Africa at this or any future point in time.

The African vision that emerged out of the Kericho workshop was based on several assumptions different from those contained in what constitutes the current perspective on Africa. These differences can be summarized with regard to policy, research and action, as follows:

DIFFERENCES BETWEEN THE AFRICAN VISION AND THE CURRENT PERSPECTIVE ON AFRICA

Level	Conventional Wisdom	African Vision
Conceptual	• unilinear • crisis-oriented	• dialectic • beyond crisis
Methodological	• surprise-free • deductive • predictive	• surprise-rich • inductive • retroductive
Institutional	• state-centred • concentrated • monopolistic	• grassroots-oriented • multiple and dispersed • pluralizing
Operational	• donor-fed and controlled • directive; pre-emptive • capital-intensive	• locally owned and initiated • supportive; nurturing • people intensive
Financial	• massive transfer • project-specific	• seed money • matching funds

Participants agreed that the various elements associated with the African vision should be further explored and propagated among researchers, analysts, and decision-makers. To that end, the participants also agreed on the need for continued networking. Africa's intellectuals need to make a more substantive contribution to the development of the continent. Much of that can be achieved if these intellectuals agree to adopt a longer-term perspective on what is happening on the continent and apply some of the approaches and methodologies identified above. Given the heavy influence that external organizations are bound to have on Africa, at least in the short and medium run, these people must also take a greater responsibility in "educating" donors and other parties concerned about the value of thinking of alternative scenarios and ways of reaching them. Policy thinking has been very sterile in recent years and a broadening of the debate is strongly called for.

Part 2

The Conventional Wisdom: A Summary

3

Projecting the Current Perspective: 1957-2057

Introduction

What will Africa look like in the year 2057—a century After Ghana initiated the wave of political independence in sub-Saharan Africa? This chapter sketches a "current perspective" scenario of development in sub-Saharan Africa until the middle of the twenty-first century. It is based on a critical review of long-term forecasts of African development published by the World Bank, the United Nations, and other organizations. The future scenario of Africa that emerges from this review is "surprise-free" in that it does not attempt to encompass specific events, unexpected changes, or other surprises that could significantly alter long-term trends. The scenario specifically excludes normative elements, as embodied, for example, in the targets for economic development set by the Lima Declaration and Plan of Action on Industrial Development and Co-operation, the International Development Strategy for the Third United Nations Development Decade, and the Lagos Plan of Action. Nor does it include the elements of prospective analysis as contained in the Interfutures Project of the Organization for Economic Co-operation and Development (OECD), whereby different futures are imagined that could result from the behaviour of individual governments acting within the existing world system.[1] A basic assumption of the scenario is that the structure of the current world economic and political system remains essentially the same. No single problem—environmental, economic, or social – proves totally intractable, nor do any technological miracles emerge that fundamentally change the relationship between humans and their resources and environment.

The focus of the scenario, as reflected in the documents from which it is created, is on conventional indicators of development such as population growth, Gross Domestic Product (GPD), and food production per capita. These are variables that are relatively easy to factor into forecasting models. As such, they are generally used to· quantify differences in development paths among the nations of the world.

This chapter, however, goes further by providing baseline data for key indicators of energy consumption, environmental change, technological capabilities, and social development, thereby providing a fuller analysis of the conventional wisdom than is usually contained in any single document. To place the African data in its proper international perspective, data are, as much as possible, provided on other developing regions and on countries or sub-regions of Africa. As a result, the reader can make comparative assessments of the degree of heterogeneity, present or projected.[2]

1. The Current Perspective

1.1 The Current Perspective and Present Trends

Current perspectives on trends in Africa are gloomy, shaped by stark pictures of misery, starvation, and death in many areas in recent years. Buttressed by discouraging statistics on recent economic performance, social development, and environmental degradation, a consensus has emerged that Africa is a continent in serious trouble. The UN General Assembly refers to the "critical economic situation" in Africa; the World Bank to "the human disaster of 1983-4...return(ing) to haunt the world community"; the US-based Committee on African Development Strategies to "the depths of the continent's fundamental development crisis"; and African governmental Ministers to "Africa's economic and social crisis".[3] These pessimistic prognoses have led many to call for dramatic changes in present social, economic, institutional, and political trends and for reorientation of current policies and development priorities.

Much of the current pessimism stems from the failure of many African countries to regain the momentum of economic growth lost in the worldwide recession of the early 1980s. In the two previous decades, sub-Saharan Africa had increased its GDP by more than 3 per cent per year on average. But the recession brought economic growth to a halt —indeed, GPD decreased by 2.6 per cent in 1983. Per capita GDP fell by 17 per cent from 1980 to 1985. In 1985, GDP increased only 1.2 per cent, despite two years of recovery in industrial market countries.[4] External public debt grew rapidly through the 1970s and early 1980s, reaching by 1984 an accumulated total equivalent to over half of the Gross National Product (GNP) of low-income sub-Saharan nations. Service on this debt itself rose to almost 4 per cent of GNP in

1984 and 14 per cent of export earnings for these nations, with even higher percentages reported in low-income African economies.[5] At the same time, gross domestic investment and most industrial production stagnated.[6]

Other indicators have been equally discouraging. The sub-Saharan population has probably risen more than 3 per cent per year since the beginning of the decade. However, continuing the trend from the 1970s, total food production failed to keep up, leading to an 8 per cent decline in per capita food production from 1980 to 1984. The number of calories available per capita declined 4 per cent during this period, despite increased agricultural imports and decreased exports.[7] At the same time, degradation of the environmental resource base for agriculture has become more noticeable. Over 80 per cent of the productive drylands of Africa are reportedly subject to moderate to very severe desertification, characterized by productivity decreases of 25 per cent or more. Rates of soil erosion and deforestation as high as several per cent per year have been reported in a number of countries.[8]

1.2 The Current Perspective and Africa's Future

Clearly, continuation of these trends into the future would be disastrous for most of Africa. The Africa of 2057 could have more than 2000 million people, four times the present population, even assuming a drastic reduction in population growth rates (to less than 1 per cent by 2055).[9] Just maintaining acceptable standards of living could be difficult, if environmental resources are permitted to degrade and non-renewable resources are consumed. Improving living standards for the bulk of the population might be impossible.

However, the current perspective is not only that a Malthusian nightmare of this kind is likely if present trends continue, but also that it can be averted. Population growth will slow due to the so-called "demographic transition" experienced on other continents; economic development can regain the momentum of the 1960s; agricultural research will generate the substantial improvements in crop yields needed to support both larger populations and improved nutrition; and environmental degradation can be limited and even reversed.

In essence, the current perspective embodies a three-stage trajectory for Africa's long-term development: a time of euphoria, a time of troubles, and a time of renewal. "Euphoria" took hold during the first decade or two after independence, when economies were booming and the social and political landscapes were open and optimistic. "Troubles" began with the well publicized famines of the 1970s and continued with a string of economic, environmental, and social setbacks that quashed optimism and helped promulgate a crisis mentality. "Renewal" will occur once the present crisis is overcome through concerted efforts by African countries and the international community.

1.3 Projecting the Current Perspective

The three-stage trajectory described above is employed in projecting the current perspective for Africa to 2057. The time of euphoria begins in 1957 and ends in 1980; the time of troubles continues to 2000; and the time of renewal extends to 2057. For many variables, each time period implies a different growth rate (see notes to Table 1, p. 32). A few variables are projected at constant rates from the present to 2057, since the conventional wisdom appears to suggest that they are relatively independent of these larger assumptions. Demographic projections are taken directly from standard World Bank and UN forecasts. Existing agricultural, energy, and other projections are used when appropriate.

The "current perspective" scenario for Africa in 2057 is summarized in section 2. More detailed descriptions of current trends and future expectations are given in sections 3-7. At the outset, however, it is useful to emphasize three important limitations that are built into this scenario.

The first limitation, inherent in most projections of the future, pertains to the accuracy and representativeness of presently available data on Africa. Statistical summaries of key demographic and economic indicators are reproduced widely in both technical and popular literature. Unfortunately, the proliferation of such summaries tends to conceal the limited quantity and quality of the primary data on which these indicators are based and the often considerable uncertainty they incorporate. Possible pitfalls include: the tendency to focus on conventional variables for which data exist, rather than on more pivotable or newly identified variables for which data are sparse; the tendency to concentrate on aggregate behaviour, rather than on the potentially more sensitive behaviour of sub-regions or sub-groups; and the tendency to ignore the

PROJECTING THE CURRENT PERSPECTIVE 31

Table 1: Summary of the "Current Perspectives" scenario for Africa, 1957-2057

SELECTED INDICATORS	ESTIMATED AND PROJECTED VALUES		
	1957	1987	2057
Demographic Variables			
Total population (million)[a]	263	599	2,154
Population growth rate (%/year)[a]	2.3	3.1	0.5
Life mortality rate (per 1,000)[a,b]	180	101	12
Life expectancy at birth (years)[a,c]	40	53	76
Level of urbanization (%)[d]	18	31	75
Economic Variables			
GDP per capita (1980 $US)[c]	440	815	3,800
Capital goods production (million 1975 $US)	133	1,273	75,800
Agricultural production (FAO index)[g]	66	115	1,072
Food supply per capital (calories)[h]	2,095	2,294	3,252
Human Resource Variables			
Literacy rate (%)[i]	15	53	80
Scientists and engineers in R&D (per million inhabitants)	13	103	266
Natural Resources and Environmental Variables			
Arable land (million ha)[k]	176	221	360
Energy consumption per capita (pkg coal equivalent per person)	172	451	2,069
Forested area (million ha)[m]	1,544	1,315	935

Notes to table 1

a. World Bank standard projection
b. Deaths per 100 live births (both sexes)
c. Both sexes
d. Value for 2057 based on linear extrapolation
e. Assumes growth rates of 2.4% per year for 1950-80, 1% for 1980-2000, and 2.5% for 2000-2057.
f. Assumes growth rates of 9.3% per year for 1957-80, 3.9% per year for 1980-2000, and 6.5% for 2000-2057
g. FAO Index of total agricultural production (1979-81 = 100). Assumed growth rates of 1.7% per year of 1957-80, 3.4% per year for 1980-2000 (at the year 2000 Scenario B) and 3.2% per year for 2000-2057.
h. Assumes growth rates of 0.4% per year for 1957-80 and 0.5% per year for 1980-2057 (at the year 2000 Scenario B).
i. Assumes that the adult literacy rate in 2057 is determined primarily by the enrolment ratio projected for the 6-11 year age group in 2000 (who will be 63-68 in 2057). Other values by linear extrapolation from rates given in World Tables: The Third Edition.
j. Assumes growth rates of 14% per year for 1957-76 and 4% per year for 1977-2057 and uses UNIDO value of 28,000 scientists and engineers in 1973. The 14% rate of increase actually implies only 7 new scientists and engineers per million inhabitants in 1973. This compares with the 1,390 students in higher education per million inhabitants estimated for 1980 in Africa.
k. Assumes growth rates of 0.8% per year for 1957-75 and about 0.7% per year 1975-2057 (at the year 2000 Scenario B).
i. Assumes growth rates of 5.5% per year for 1957-70, 1.5% per year for 1970-85, and 2.2% per year for 1986-2057.
m. Assumes reduction rate of 0.5% per year for 1957-2057.

effects of uncertainty on extrapolations into the future. Thus, although these data certainly have uses, it is important to keep their problems in mind in thinking about the future.

A second limitation is that at best the forecasts of the future used in the scenario consider only a few key variables at a time. Few consider possible interactions between variables or important heterogeneities in any detail. For example, almost all economic and social forecasts treat demographic projects as an external or "exogenous" input, thereby limiting the potential feedback of social and economic factors to demographic behaviour. The demographic projections themselves incorporate gross assumptions about future economic and social conditions and about the effects of these on demographic behaviour. Such assumptions are usually varied to a limited degree to produce "low", "medium", and "high" estimates, but this procedure may mask the effects of complex interactions and feedbacks characteristic of many real systems. The current perspective is essentially a tunnel vision of the future in which at present there is very little light. It is likely to overlook important self-regulatory mechanisms, thresholds, or other non-linear phenomena and therefore may fail to characterize fully the range of possible futures. What may seem implausible today could well be common practice tomorrow.

A third limitation is that the current perspective still operates on the assumption, originally derived from the modernization theory in the 1950s and 1960s, that anything that runs counter to the economically rational is an obstacle to be removed. Indigenous cultural values, for instance, tend to be regarded as outdated and due to be changed at any cost. The inevitable outcome has been disrespect and disregard for anything African, and the emergence of a "top-down" approach to development. The nature and quality of social interaction as well as human creativity and self-esteem tend to be ignored in this perspective.

With these cautions in mind, it is useful to summarize what Africa may look like in 2057 based on the extrapolation of current perspectives into the future.

2. Africa in 2057

In 2057, Africa is a continent of 2 billion people, one-fifth of the world's total population, with an average per capita income of $3,800 and an average life expectancy of 76, with almost all of its children in primary school and half in secondary school, and with intensive use of its rich natural resources (Table 1, p. 31). As such, it is about as densely populated, as wealthy, healthy, and educated, and as environmentally transformed as Greece was in the early 1980s (Table 2, p. 34).

More than half of the African population is concentrated in eastern

34 BEYOND HUNGER IN AFRICA

Table 2: For variables, comparison between the "Current Perspective" scenario for Africa in 2057 and actual data for Greece in the early 1980s.

SELECTED INDICATORS	AFRICA IN 2057	GREECE IN 1980-85
Demographic Variables		
Population density (per km²)	73	74
Total fertility rate (per 1,000)	2.07	2.15
Crude birth rate (per 1,000)	14.1	14.9
Crude death rate (per 1,000)	9.3	10.1
Infant mortality rate (per 1,000)	12	16
Life expectancy at birth (years)	76	74
Population aged 0-14 (%)	22.4	22.2
Population aged 65 (%)	9.5	13.1
Level of urbanization (%)	75	59
Economic Variables		
GDP per capita (1980 US$)	3,800	3,790c
Capital goods production per capita (millions 1975 US$ per capita)	35	57d
Food supply per capita (calories)	3,252	3,627e
Human Resources Variables		
Literacy rate (%)	80	92.3f
Scientists and engineers in R&D (per million inhabitants)	266	279g
Natural Resource and Environmental Variables		
Arable land (ha/person)	0.15	0.4e
Energy consumption per capita (kg coal equivalent per person)	2,069	2,092h

Notes to Table 2

a. See notes to Table 1. Demographic data from Vu (1985)
b. 1980-85 average except as noted. Demographic data from UN (1986a)
c. 1980-81 average based on UNIDO (1985) data. The 1981 GDP value was converted to 1980 dollars using the GDP deflator from World Bank (1983b)
d. 1975 data (UNIDO, 1985)
e. 1980-84 average (FAO, 1986f)
f. Estimated 1985 value (UNESCO, 1985)
g. 1979 value (UNESCO, 1985)
h. 1980-83 average (UN, 1985c)

and Western Africa. In all regions, population growth has slowed substantially. Less than one-fourth of the population is under 15 years of age. Three-quarters of the population live in urban areas, with perhaps a third of these in cities of over 4 million people.

Average per capita incomes have risen almost fivefold since 1987. Both agriculture and industry have expanded rapidly. Agricultural production has increased more than ninefold, raising per capita food supplies by almost half. Although not self-sufficient in meeting its industrial demands, Africa does produce capital goods equal in value to what the United Kingdom was producing in 1980.

Children born in 2057 have a life expectancy of 76 years. Mortality among infants has dropped to the level in North America in the 1980s. Relatively few children will have more than one sibling. Most will receive primary education and probably secondary education, and almost all will learn to read. As adults, they will have good opportunities for higher education, technical training, and subsequent employment within Africa.

Greatly expanded agricultural and industrial production, high-density population clusters, and rapidly growing energy consumption continue to place tremendous pressures on natural resources and the environment. Although the worst problems of soil erosion, deforestation, and desertification have been contained, many areas still face serious losses and must make substantial investments to keep them under control. Attempts to deal with localized pollution problems have generally been successful, but the threat of large-scale hazards such as radioactive or biological contamination is growing.

This snapshot of Africa's future is based on projections of the current perspective, a perspective that is most definite about population growth, sets the initial stage for economic growth and human resource development, and provides ambiguous and contradictory signs about environmental and social change. Clearly, it neglects many possible feedbacks and interactions among demographic, economic, environmental, and social changes that could significantly alter Africa's future. For example, the current perspective says very little about what appear to be increasing inter- and intra-regional disparities in population growth and economic development that could spur increased migration, political instability, armed conflict, or other "surprises". By the same token, in relying primarily on extrapolations of recent performance, it tends to exclude possibilities for more rapid development such as that experienced by Japan, the USSR and other countries in recent decades.

Also, it is an average projection, ignoring the great diversity in population density, living standards, and other characterists found in Africa today. If this present diversity were maintained into the future, then in 2057 the majority of nation-states would actually be below the average in many indicators. Thus, for example, the ten or so poorest countries with about one-fourth of the African population would still have average per capita GDPs below $1,200. Half of the population would live in 29 countries with GDP per capita of $3,000 or less.[10] One-tenth of the population would be concentrated in 5 countries with densities in excess of 470 people per square km.[11]

The five countries are Nigeria, Burundi, Rwanda, the Comoros and Mauritius. How would this "current perspective" scenario evolve? The following sections review some of the basic demographic, economic and resource trends since 1957 in Africa and current expectations for the future to 2057.

3. Demographic Expectations

3.1 Population

In 1955, sub-Saharan Africa [12] had a population of 190 million people, 7% of the world total. By 1985, this population had more than doubled to 432 million. Recent UN and World Bank studies predict another doubling by 2010, raising the proportion of the world's population in sub-Saharan Africa to over 13%! A third doubling, to 1,700 million people, could occur by 2055.

Most of this population growth is expected to take place in Eastern and Western Africa (Figure 1), where more than half of Africa's population currently resides and where overall fertility rates remain high. In the UN "medium variant" projection, annual growth rates in these two regions exceed 3% per year in the next century and then decline rapidly to about 2% by 2025 (Figure 2). As a result, East and West Africa almost quadruple their 1980 populations by 2025, whereas Northern and Southern Africa grow by less than a factor of 3. Nigeria, now the tenth largest country in the world with a population of 95 million, could replace the United States as the fourth largest by 2025 (see Table 3).[13]

Figure 1. Estimated and projected population by region of Africa, 1950-2025, UN medium variant. See Table 3 for countries in each region. Source: UN, 1986.

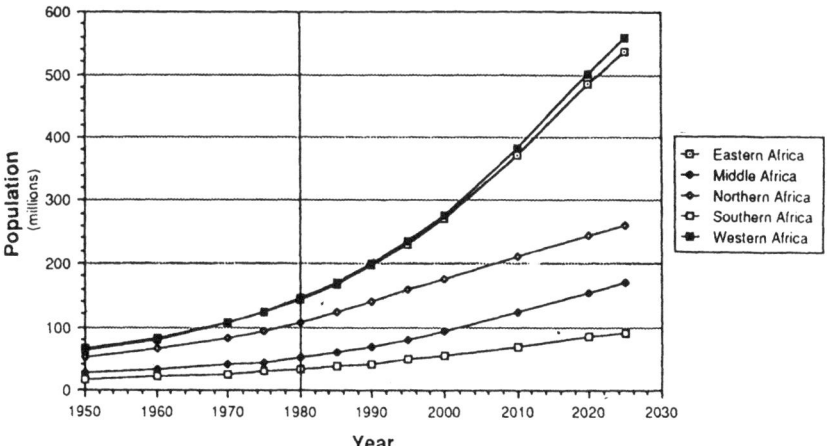

38 BEYOND HUNGER IN AFRICA

Fig. 2. Estimated and projected population growth rates by region of Africa, 1950-2025, UN medium variant. See Table 3 for countries in each region. Source: UN, 1986.

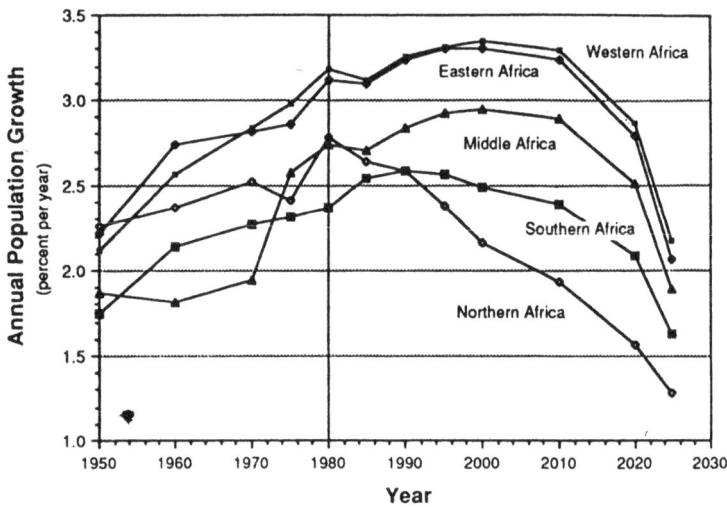

Table 3. African population estimates (thousands). Sources: UN, 1986a; Vu, 1985.

COUNTRY OR AREA	UN ESTIMATE	UN MEDIUM VARIANT	WORLD BANK STANDARD PROJECTION
	1985	2025	2055
Total Africa	554,928	1,616,516	2,131,675
Eastern Africa	166,404	36,859	690,925
British Indian Ocean Territory	2	2	—
Burundi	4,721	11,817	19,329
Comoros	444	1,046	1,739
Djibouti	364	1,203	1,852
Ethiopia	43,557	122,285	148,179

PROJECTING THE CURRENT PERSPECTIVE 39

Kenya	20,600	82,850	100,938
Madagascar	110,012	28,120	43,973
Malawi	6,944	21,855	30,014
Mauritius	1,050	1,606	1,836
Mozambique	13,961	37,154	56,325
Reúnion	531	812	933
Rwanda	6,070	20,212	31,186
Seychelles	76	252	128[a]
Somalia	4,653	12,191	23,944
Uganda	15,477	55,190	67,237
United Republic of Tanzania	22,499	83,805	101,167
Zambia	6,666	23,799	27,892
Zimbabwe	8,777	32,658	34,253
Middle Africa	**59,538**	**169,597**	**238,585**
Angola	8,754	24,484	33,837
Cameroon	9,874	27,763	43,486
Central African Republic	2,576	6,339	9,883
Chad	5,018	12,356	17,413
Congo	1,740	4,732	8,111
Equatorial Guinea	392	937	1,191
Gabon	1,151	2,607	3,078
Sao Tomé/Principe	97	284	330
Zaire	29,938	90,097	121,256

[a] The World Bank's estimate for 2025 is 110,000

Northern Africa	**122,960**	**260,767**	**373,356**
Algeria	21,718	50,611	92,167
Egypt	46,909	90,399	103,656
Libyan Arab Jamahiriya	3,605	11,090	16,035
Morocco	21,941	40,062	60,912
Sudan	21,550	55,379	82,753
Tunisia	7,081	12,860	17,234
Western Sahara	155	365	599

Southern Africa	37,218	90,991	110,908
Botswana	1,107	4,151	3,925[a]
Lesotho	1,520	3,877	5,129
Namibia	1,550	4,474	4,308[b]
South Africa	32,392	76,381	94,567
Swaziland	650	2,107	2,979
Western Africa	168,808	558,302	717,888
Benin	4,050	12,701	16,774
Burkina Faso	6,942	20,106	24,419
Cape Verde	326	712	1,056
Cote d'Ivoire	9,810	29,978	39,873
Gambia	643	1,494	2,527
Ghana	13,588	47,020	55,355
Guinea	6,075	15,561	18,470
Guinea-Bissau	889	2,014	2,747
Liberia	2,191	7,517	8,916
Mali	8,082	24,142	29,259
Mauritania	1,888	5,780	6,608
Niger	6,115	18,940	30,821
Nigeria	95,198	338,105	431,256
St/Helena	6	19	13
Senegal	6,444	17,872	24,384
Sierra Leone	3,602	7,416	12,743
Togo	2,960	8,923	12,680

*Previous census prior to 1975

[a]The World Bank's estimate for 2025 is 2,902,000
[b]The World Bank's estimate for 2025 is 3,132,000

The age structure of the African population is expected to change significantly by 2055, according to projected World Bank age distributions for all of Africa. In sub-Saharan Africa, the childhood dependency ratio (the ratio of those under 15 to those aged 15-64) decreases slowly until the end of the century, from 88% in 1980 to 81% in 2005. It then decreases more rapidly due to declining birth rates, dropping to 47% by 2030 and to 33% by 2055. The old-age dependency ratio for the elderly (the ratio of those over 65 to those 15-64) increases only about 1% before 2030 from the 1980 level of 6%, but then jumps to 13% by 2055. The median age in Africa increases from 17 in 1980 to 31 in 2050 in the UN projections.[14]

Population estimates over the next century vary substantially among different UN and World Bank projections. In 2025, the UN high variant exceeds the medium variant by 14%, and the low variant is 18% lower. The World Bank standard estimate for 2025 is 10% less that the corresponding UN medium-variant estimate. In 2050, the World Bank estimates vary about +12% from the standard estimate of 1,700 million, depending on whether fertility declines quickly or slowly. Thus, based on these estimates, by 2057 there could be as few as 1,200 million people in sub-Saharan Africa or as many as 2,200 million.

Differences in the projections stem primarily from different assumptions about future fertility trends. The UN medium variant assumes that the total fertility rate (TFR) for Africa falls to 6 children per woman in the early 1990s and to 3.2 by 2020-5. In the high variant, the TFR averages 6 in 1985-90, and declines to 2.4 by 2020-5. In the World Bank standard projection, the TFR drops below 6 by 1995 and below 3 by 2025. In the "rapid fertility decline" case, the drop in fertility is assumed to occur 15 years earlier than in the standard case, and in the "slow fertility decline" case, 10 years later. Other uncertainties arise from differences about migration and mortality and from the poor quality of initial population estimates.[15]

The UN considers the medium variant to be representative of "future demographic trends that seem likely to occur". The high and low variants are intended to "indicate the plausible range of future deviations from the medium-variant projections", although, it is cautioned, this range is not necessarily "exhaustive". It is noteworthy, however, that current estimates for 1985 place the African population above even the high-variant estimates of prior assessments, i.e. above what was considered "plausible" just a few years before.[16]

3.2 Fertility

The most important contributor to the high population growth expected for Africa is the fertility rate, which has persisted at the level of 6.5 births per woman in the decades since 1950. The highest recorded fertility of any country is in Kenya, where there were 8.3 births per woman on average in 1970-7. The lowest fertility in Africa is in Mauritius, where the TFR decreased from 3.5 births per woman in 1974 to 2.9 in 1980.[17] In ten countries of sub-Saharan Africa, only 3-4% of married women of childbearing age use modern forms of contraception, compared with 50% or more in many parts of Asia. This region is also unique in that the desired family size apparently exceeds the total fertility rate, according to survey data from the mid-1970s [18].

Historic and projected fertility rates by world region are shown in Figure 3 (UN medium variant). The so-called "demographic transition" is clearly evident in the rapid drop of East Asian fertility rates in the past two decades and appears to be underway in Latin America and South Asia. It is projected to repeat itself throughout Africa over the next century.

Figure 3. Historical and projected fertility rates by world region (U.N. medium variant)

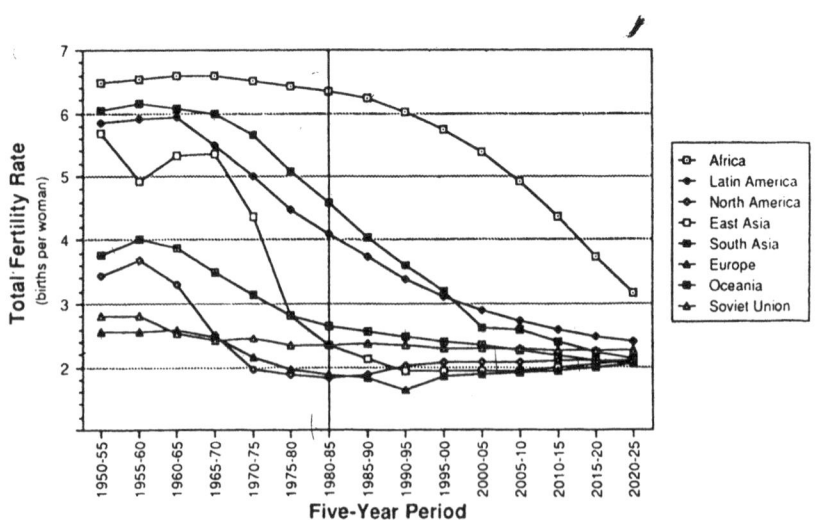

Unfortunately, there is much uncertainty as to what factors affect the magnitude and rate of fertility decline. Known influences include age, nuptiality, urban versus rural residence, educational level, participation of women in the labour force, contraceptive use, and desired family size. Only a few of these are explicitly taken into consideration in the UN and World Bank projections[19].

3.3 Mortality

Mortality rates have dropped significantly in Africa in recent decades. Crude death rates have decreased almost 40% since 1950, to 16.6 deaths per 1,000 people in 1980-5. Life expectancy at birth has increased by almost 12 years, from an average of only 37.8 years in 1950-5 to 49.4 years in 1980-5. Life expectancies by country range from 31 years measured in a 1963-4 survey in Chad to 67 years on the island of Mauritius in 1980[20].

However, Africa lags behind other regions of the world in both the level of mortality and the rate of mortality improvement. In south Asia, life expectancy is now more than 5 years greater than in Africa, having increased by some 15 years during the 1950-85 period. East Asian life expectancy grew by 26 years during the same period, a phenomenal increase of 60% that moved the region from sixth to fourth in rank among eight world regions. These differences in mortality and mortality reduction between world regions are expected to persist in the next several decades.

Mortality projections by the UN and World Bank are generally based on observed rates of improvement in life expectancy at birth. However, in developing countries mortality data are poor, so the UN assumes that life expectancy increases by 2.5 years during every five-year period up to 62.5 years, after which gains are smaller. In some sub-Saharan countries, the quinquennial gains are reduced to 2 years or less as warranted by recent evidence. The same pattern is used in all three UN variants. According to the UN, life expectancy in Africa as a whole will therefore reach 64.5 years by 2020-25[21]. The World Bank projections take into account current life expectancy and female primary school enrolment. According to the World Bank, life expectancy in Africa as a whole will reach 67 years by 2020-25 and 72 by 2030-55[22].

The infant mortality rate (IMR) has declined one-third since 1950, from 184 deaths per thousand births to 116 in 1980-5, according to UN estimates. The greatest decline occurred in the island nation of Réunion, which reduced its IMR from 140 to 19 during this period. Only Réunion and Mauritius have IMRs under 50. Rates above 100 per thousand persist in 34 nations, with at least two of these (Sierra Leone and Burkina Faso) exceeding 200 per thousand. In 14 sub-Saharan countries with reliable trend data, the rate of decline has averaged less than 2% per year.[23]

UN projections of the IMR are based on the annual rates of increase in life expectancy at birth given above and on an assumed age pattern of mortality change. Thus, the projected African IMR shows an almost linear decrease to 50 deaths per thousand births by 2025. Twenty-three countries, of which more than half are in West Africa, are expected to have IMRs above 50 at that time, but only three of these above 100. Similarly, the World Bank projects an African IMR of only 42 in 2025 and 23 in 2055.[24]

3.4 Urbanization

Africa is still predominantly rural, with only one-third of its population living in urban areas, compared with more than two-thirds in the developed world and Latin America. Within Africa, southern and northern Africa are the most urbanized and eastern and western Africa the least.

Urbanization has proceeded rapidly in Africa in the past few decades, although only at half the rate experienced by Latin America and the Soviet Union. Middle Africa has had the most rapid urban growth, averaging about 0.7% per year for the last two decades. Some cities have shown remarkable growth. For example, Nairobi in Kenya, Abidjan in the Ivory Coast, and Dar es Salaam in Tanzania have grown more than sixfold since 1950. Lagos, Nigeria, grew 16-fold during the same period. Between 1957 and 1977, Nouakchott, the capital of Mauritania, developed from a village of 2,000 into a city of 134,000, a 60-fold increase. Niamey, the capital of Niger, expanded from 7,000 to 300,000 inhabitants between 1945 and 1979[25].

Urbanization is expected to accelerate in the future, with natural increase playing a growing role. By 2025, Southern Africa is projected to reach the level of urbanization that presently exists in the developed world and Latin America. About half of the population of eastern and western Africa will live in urban areas at that time. In absolute terms, this means that the urban populations of the five African regions will increase from 4 to 12 times above their 1980 levels by 2025[26]. Much of this growth is expected to take place in much larger urban conglomerations than presently exist. In 1980, only northern Africa had a significant proportion of its urban population residing in cities of 4 million or more inhabitants. The Cairo/Giza/Imbaba area in Egypt was the only African urban agglomeration to rank among the 35 largest of the world. By 2025, however, 10-40% of the urban populations in all five regions are projected to live in cities of 4 million or more. Kinshasa, Zaire and Lagos, Nigeria will join the ranks of the 35 largest agglomerations with over 8 million people each in the year 2000. This unprecedented urban growth could have far reaching effects on fertility, employment, education, agriculture, political stability, and other demographic and socio-economic factors.[27]

4. Economic Performance

As noted previously, poor economic performance in sub-Saharan Africa in recent years is a major source of pessimism about Africa's future in the long term. If per capita production stagnates or declines, there will be little room for the significant improvements in education, health, and living standards that, it is believed, are fundamental to reducing population growth rates. Debt and trade problems would worsen and the growth of agriculture would be constrained. Unemployment and underemployment would increase, perhaps leading to increased political discontent. A "vicious cycle of economic deterioration and political instability"[28] could ensue.

Unfortunately, there has been relatively little rigorous analysis of long-term economic development in Africa. Most projections have been made only one to two decades into the future. Most have looked at only a few aggregate indicators of gross production, agriculture, and industry for the continent as a whole or for one or two sub-groupings of countries. Virtually all take population growth and other demographic trends as given.

4.1 Gross Production

The Gross Domestic Product (GDP) measures the output of domestically produced goods and services. In 1950, African GDP (including North Africa) was US$373 per capita in 1980, 2-3 times larger than East and South Asian per capita GDP, but 2-7 times smaller than that in Latin America and the developed countries (Table 4). By 1980, per capita GDP had doubled, but the gap between Africa and the developed world had increased in both absolute and relative terms. Even by the year 2000 per capita GDP in Africa will not reach the estimated level that the developed countries had attained one century earlier[29].

Future economic growth in developed and developing nations is generally determined exogenously, based on past economic performance

Table 4: Estimated and projected per capita GDP for world regions, 1900-2000, using two methods. Units are dollars of 1980 purchasing power. Source: McGreevey, 1985.

Year	Africa	Southeast and East Asia	South Asia	Western Asia	Developed Countries	Latin America
a) Exchange Rate Method						
1900	190	125	132	400	1,404	420
1950	373	128	154	1,000	2,741	900
1980	760	290	240	5,500	8,441	1,886
2000	927	475	323	6,700	11,370	2,800
b) Purchasing-power Parity Method						
1900	320	300	320	280	1,322	600
1950	451	306	340	700	2,580	1,257
1980	925	660	510	3,870	6,000	2,715
2000	1,130	1,081	686	4,710	8,082	4,030

and expectations or goals for future performance. A widespread assumption is that growth rates in developing countries are closely tied to those in industrial countries. For example, the *World Development Report 1984* posits a law case intended to indicate "what might happen if the industrial countries were to do nothing to improve their performance of the past ten years." GDP growth during 1985-95 in these countries is assumed to drop to 2.5% per year on average. Then "slow growth in the industrial countries would limit GDP growth in the developing countries to an average of only 4.7% per year, and to only 2.7% per year in per capita terms." For low-income Africa, the 1984 projection for GDP growth is only 2.8% leading to a decline in GDP per capita of 0.5% per year during 1985-95, but prospects for Africa were not seen as much better—GDP increases only 3.2% per year and per capita GDP declines 0.1% per year—due to the poor "market outlook for these countries' commodity exports".[30]

Recent declines in oil prices and interest rates are viewed as a stimulus to many developing countries, so that the more recent *World Development Report 1986* shows increased optimism about economic growth in low-income countries. In the low-income case, GDP in low-income African countries increases 3.2% per year in 1985-95, and per capita GDP stays at present levels. In the high case, GDP grows at an average of 4.0% per year and per capita GDP 0.8% per year. West and Central Africa grow faster in both absolute and per capita terms.[31] Growth rates in other developing countries are predicted to be 1-4% higher, principally because, in the World Bank's view:

Developing countries that attempt to insulate themselves from the world economy may reduce the impact of international cycles, but they pay the high price of lower growth rates under any world scenario[32].

These World Bank projections appear rather pessimistic in comparison with "historical trend" scenarios developed by various UN organizations. In a 1983 report on Africa's development through 2008, the UN ECA projected an average GDP growth rate for all of Africa of 5.3% per year in its "gloomy" historical trend scenario. A 1983 study by the UN Industrial Development Organization (UNIDO) anticipated a growth rate of 6.2% per year in all developing countries, implying a 2.5% per year increase in per capita GDP in the developing countries of Africa over 1980-2000. Per capita GDP in these countries increased from $465 to $755 (1975 US dollars)[33]. Under an accelerated-growth scenario, which follows the targets set in the International Developing Strategy for the Third United Nations Development Decade, the GDP grows 7.0% per year in developing countries, implying a 3.9% per year increase in per capita GDP to $1,005 by the year 2000 (Figure 4). Clearly, there is a significant gap between the expectations of institutions like the World Bank that apparently weigh recent economic performance heavily and the expectations and aspirations of institutions like the UN that seem to reflect a more historical, medium-term view of development progress.

Figure 4. Estimated and projected GDP per capita in the developed and developing worlds, 1980-2000. Source: UNIDO, 1983.

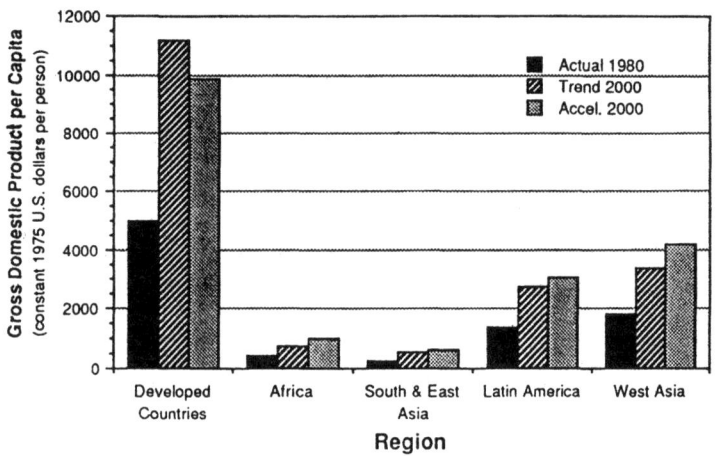

A basic weakness of these projections is that future rates of economic growth are specified exogenously, based on the subjective judgements of analysts. An alternative is to model economic relationships explicitly, allowing growth rates to be computed endogenously, that is, as a consequence rather than as a cause of economic change. Unfortunately, the methodologies available for this type of modelling are presently rather limited.

One effort along these lines has been made by Leontief et al., who developed a multi-regional input-output model of the world economy with economic growth rates treated endogenously. Population growth is prescribed, and there are no feedbacks between economic and demographic factors. Over the period 1970-2000, the model projects average annual growth in per capita GDP of 1.5-1.9% per year in the "resource-poor" developing countries (arid Africa and parts of Asia and Latin America) and about 5.9% in the "resource-rich" developing countries (tropical and northern Africa, the Middle East, and low-income Latin America). By 2000, GDP averages $290-330 (1970 US dollars) in the resource-poor region and $1,530 – 1,630 in the resource-rich region. A later version of the model projects per capita GDP as growing 1.5-2.5% per year from 2000-2030 in the resource-poor region, reaching $440-630 in 2030, and 0.8-2.1% per year in the resource-rich region, reaching $1,940-3,370 in 2030.[34]

A different approach was taken in the Interfutures Project. This study postulated changing economic relationships among developed countries and between the north and south. In the scenario most pessimistic with respect to GDP growth in Africa, north-south confrontation intensifies, and developing countries try to reduce their dependence on the north. In another scenario, polarization in both developed and developing countries increases, leading to reduced free trade between major zones of influences. The most optimistic scenarios envision expansion in north-south trade and sustained economic growth in the developed countries. GDP projections for the year 2000 were made for each scenario using a macroeconomic model. The resulting ranges of GDP-per-capita levels are $223-380 (1970 US dollars) in sub-Saharan African countries and $1,680-2,450 in North Africa and western Asia[35].

4.2 Manufacturing

Industrialization is generally seen as a key element of economic development. Manufacturing in sub-Saharan Africa has grown faster than the economy as a whole, and, according to one World Bank dataset, has outpaced growth in several other developing regions[36]. However, a more pessimistic picture has been painted in other World Bank and UN documents, which report that growth in manufacturing production fell to 4.9% or less during the 1970s, below that of other developing regions[37]. This significant discrepancy appears to originate mainly in the different weights used to aggregate individual-country growth rates: the *World Tables* rates are weighed by the 1976 Manufacturing Value Added (MVA), whereas the more pessimistic World Bank rates use the relative 1970 GDPs. The latter method seems suspect since it gives undue weight to those countries with large agricultural sectors but relatively small industrial bases (e.g., Ghana and Uganda) and since the bulk of manufacturing in Africa is concentrated in only a few countries[38].

Within the manufacturing sector, most production is in agriculture-related activities and light industry. It is generally believed that most such activity is devoted to producing substitutes for fairly simple consumer products that had been imported in the past. Only 8% of the MVA is attributable to the production of capital goods, and just 6% to oil refining (despite a high level of crude oil production). Even under a scenario of 'increased South-South co-operation" assessed by UÑIDO in 1985, this situation is not expected to change significantly in the near future[39].

The absolute level of production of capital goods has grown rapidly since the early 1960s. The total value added of capital goods quadrupled from 1963 to 1979, 9% per year growth rate. This compares with a 6.5% per year rate of growth for the world as a whole over the same period. The largest and fastest growth was in transportation equipment, which expanded 11% per year in 1963-79 and appears to have almost doubled in value (in real terms) from 1975-77. Africa's share of the world total value added is miniscule — less than 0.2% in 1979[40].

UNIDO has projected MVA per capita by extrapolating 1960-80 growth rates experienced by individual countries to the year 2000. The implied growth rate for developing countries is 7.9% per year[41]. In Africa MVA per capita increases by a factor of 2.5. Under the accelerated-growth scenario, it increases by 3.5. The resulting levels of MVA per capita are comparable to those in South and East Asia, but still less than those that prevailed in the rest of the world in 1980. In absolute terms, the UNIDO historical-trend scenario results in only a 15% share for the developing world in the total world MVA by the year 2000, far short of the 25% target set at the Lima Conference in 1975. The accelerated-growth scenario projects a 19.2% share. Africa's contribution increases from just 1% in 1980 to 1.2% in 2000 under the historical-trend scenario and to 2.0% under the accelerated-growth scenario. Larger increases are possible—for example, Japan increased its share from negligible levels in the early 1940s to 9% in 1980—but are not viewed as likely in Africa's case[42]. Even more pessimistic are projections of world industrial production made by the Interfutures Project, which anticipated an average growth rate of 4.6-5.4% over 1970-2000 in Black Africa. In all scenarios, the Third World share in total world MVA reaches only 16-19% by 2000, and Black Africa's share stays under 1%[43].

5. Food and Agriculture Prospects

Agriculture remains the basic industry of Africa. In low-income countries, it employs four-fifths of the labour force and generates two-fifths of the GDP. Agricultural products constitute two-thirds of total exports. Although levels of self-sufficiency have declined in recent years, agriculture still provides more than 80% of the food consumed in sub-Saharan Africa[44].

5.1 Agricultural Production

African agricultural production increased steadily through the 1960s at an average rate of 2.5% per year. In the 1970s, growth in both food and total agricultural production slowed to 1.7 and 1.4% per year, respectively, in 1970-82. In the early 1980s, production of most commodities stagnated or declined, in part due to the widespread drought beginning in 1983 that severely affected some 25 African countries. Prices for many export commodities also fell dramatically[45]. Fortunately, good weather since 1985 has permitted record high cereal production throughout Africa in recent years[46].

The agricultural statistics of the past few decades are extremely discouraging in the light of high population growth rates. Per capita agricultural production grew only 0.2% per year in 1960-70 and declined about 1% in 1970-72. Decreases in per capita food production occurred in 13 sub-Saharan countries in the 1960s and in 32 countries in the 1970s. Cereal imports increased by almost a factor of 4 in volume and over 10 in cost between 1970 and 1980. Despite such imports, however, per capita food consumption dropped somewhat, from 2,170 food calories per person per day in 1960 to 2,157 in 1981[47]. The number of people with energy-deficient diets is estimated to have grown as much as 50% in 37 sub-Saharan countries[48].

Projections of present trends into the future show little promise of near-term improvement in per capita food supplies. For example, in the *Global 2000* study, per capita food production declines in sub-Saharan Africa more than 13% by the year 2000 even in the most optimistic scenario. The 1981 FAO study, *Agriculture: Toward 2000* (AT2000), predicts a level of only 2320 calories per person per day in the year 2000 (Figure 5a). A more recent FAO study, *African Agriculture: The Next 25 Years* (AA2010), predicts stagnant supplies in West, Central, and Sahelian Africa and declines in East Africa, with increases only in northern and southern Africa. Under more optimistic assumptions, per capita food supplies may still not reach the levels now present in Latin America and the Near East by the year 2000 (Figure 5b). One result is that the absolute numbers of people affected by undernutrition could increase, although their proportion in the total population will probably decline[49].

As in the past, these declines in per capita food supplies come about primarily because population growth outstrips growth in agricultural production in Africa. In the AT2000 trend scenario, total agricultural production grows at an annual rate of 2.6%, higher than the 1961-80 average. In the most optimistic scenario, production increases over 4% per year, a rate higher than that experienced or expected in other developing regions.

Cereal production increases correspondingly (Figure 6a), but the self-sufficiency ratio for cereals (the percentage of cereal demand met by domestic production) nevertheless declines at least until 1990 (Figure 6b). Even sharper declines are projected under other scenarios. Similarly, in the AA2010 study's 'improved performance' scenario, cereal deficits increase greatly and self-sufficiency ratios stagnate, despite a projected 3% per year growth in total cereal production from 1980-2010 in sub-Saharan Africa. A further complication is the potential for greatly increased use of cereals as feed for livestock[50].

Increases in total production are attributable to three factors: increases in yields, expansion of cultivation, and intensification of land use. During the past two decades, increases in harvested area have accounted for all of the increased food output in western and central Africa and for half of the increase in eastern and southern Africa[51]. In the

Figure 5b. Estimated and projected average calorie supply in the developing world, 1964-2000. Historic values are 1961-65 and 1974-76 averages. Source: FAO, 1981.

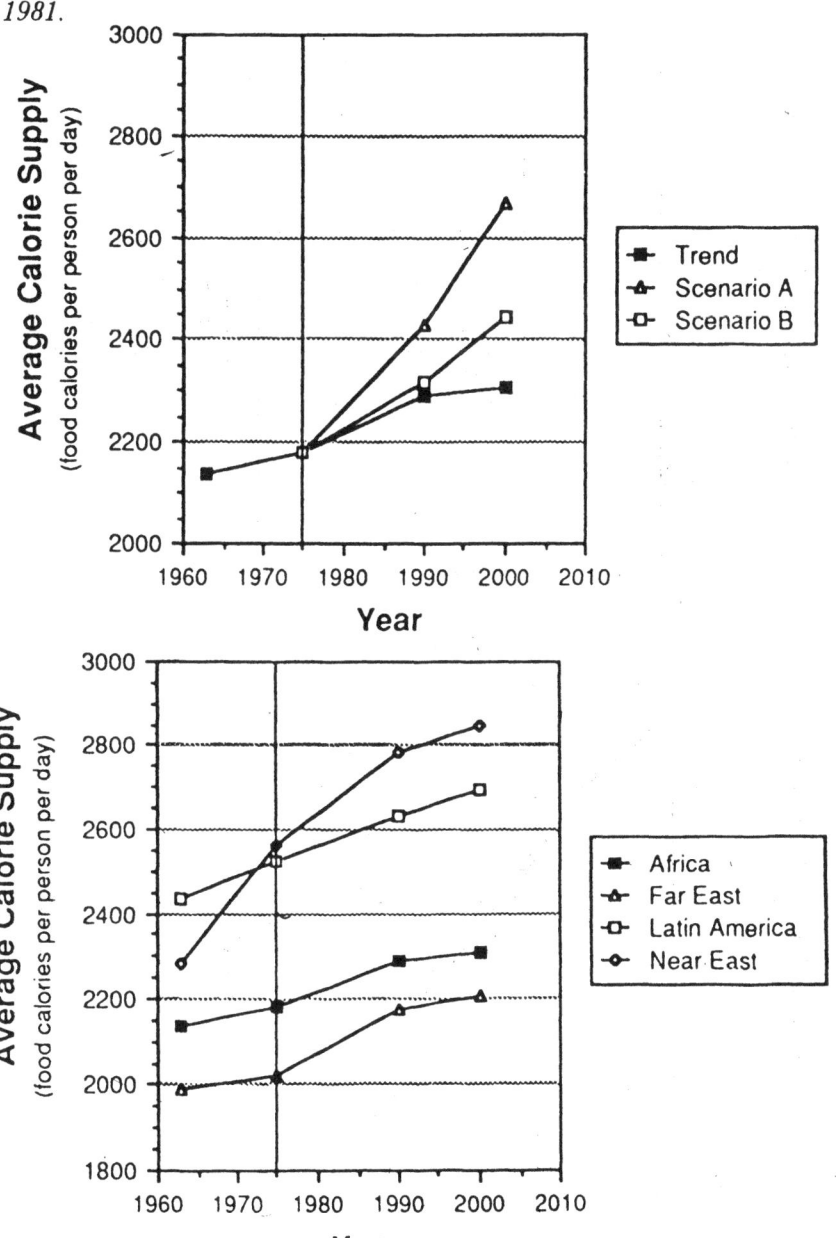

Figure 6a. Estimated and projected cereal production and self-sufficiency ratios in Africa (37 countries), 1961-2000. Historic values are 1961-65, 1968-72 and 1975-79 average. Sources: FAO, 1981.

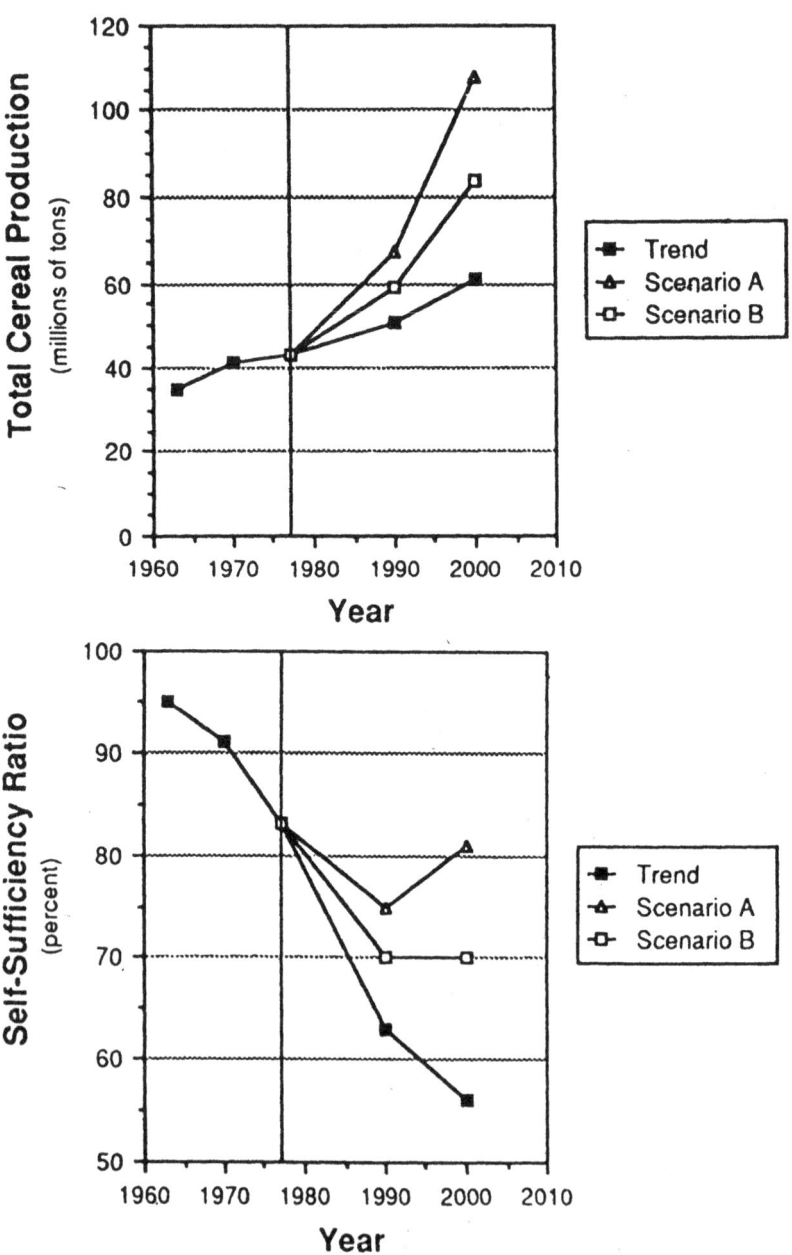

future, it is expected that improved productivity will play an increasing role. For example, in the various FAO scenarios, improved yields account for roughly half of the expected production increase, while expanded cultivation accounts for one-fourth to under one-half. In the more optimistic scenarios, increased yields dominate. Regardless, all three factors require high levels of capital investment and other inputs. Thus, it is almost universally assumed that growth rates in agricultural production are limited by growth rates in GDP.

However, most agricultural projections use exogenously determined GDP growth rates that are much higher than those reported previously. In the *Global 2000* study, the GNP growth rates for 1985-2000 that were used in the food and agriculture model simulations were significantly higher than the scenario GNP projections that were developed for the study itself[52]. In MOIRA, the Model for International Relations in Agriculture, annual average rates of 6% or more in non-agricultural GDP were assumed for tropical Africa and the Sahel during 1985-2005 in the standard case. The Regional Food Plan for Africa projects increases of 6.7% per year in African GDP over 1985-90 and 3.7% per year in GDP per capita. The AT2000 study assumes an African GDP growth rate of 6.9% per year in 1980-2000 in Scenario A and 5.4% in Scenario B. The more recent AA2010 study apparently uses the less optimistic projections of the World Bank through 1995 and then FAO extrapolations afterwards[53].

The AT2000 report concludes with a hypothetical extrapolation at the year 2055, based on the World Bank's long-range population projections and assuming that the per capita food consumption in the Developing World (including China) reaches half that in the developed World by 2055. Attaining this level will require a 3.1% per year growth rate in total agricultural demand from 1980-2000 and a 1.8% growth rate from 2000-2055. By 2055, total demand for food and agricultural products in developing countries would be five times greater than in 1980. The required rate of increase for Africa would presumably be higher. In the FAO's view, most of the increase would have to come from rapid improvement in crop and livestock yield[54].

5.2 Increases in Yield and Arable Land

Present yields in Africa are lower than in any other world region for most major food crops and are well below their estimated potential. This stems in part from the very low utilization of fertilizers and other inputs[55]. At the AT2000 study, yields of major food crops increase 45% or more in Scenario A and 30% or more in Scenario B. Nevertheless, cereal yields barely reach present levels in the Near East even in Scenario A and less than one-half of their potential level.

Further increases, to as much as two-thirds of the potential on average, could occur by the year 2030, but this assumes that there are improvements in the efficiency in the use of inputs and, in many cases, significant technological innovations.[56] The need to improve agricultural research is therefore almost universally cited as a priority. Increased fertilizer consumption over the next few decades is also emphasized. At the same time, it is generally assumed that potential threats to agriculture such as soil erosion, desertification, and deforestation can be controlled (see section 7.2).

In 1975, less than one-third of Africa's potential arable land was cultivated (Figure 7a). The rate of expansion of cultivated areas decreased from about 2.4% per year in the 1960s to only 0.8% per year between 1969-71 and 1980.[57] Over the period 1980-2000, the AT2000 study anticipates continued expansion at about 0.7% per year in Scenario B and at 1.0% per year in Scenario A. A slight slowdown is expected from 2000-2030. At these modest rates, slightly less than half of the potentially arable land would be cultivated in 2030.[58] According to FAO data, arable land per capita would decrease from 0.64 hectares per person in 1975 to 0.39 in 2000 and about 0.2 in 2030. Within Africa, arable land is not distributed evenly, with by far the largest reserves in Central and southern Africa and almost none in North Africa[59].

Irrigated agriculture is very limited in Africa relative to other developing regions, and expansion of irrigated land area is expected to be slow (Figure 7b). At present, only about 2.5% of the agricultural land is under irrigation, and much of this is concentrated in just a few countries.[60] This proportion is not expected to change significantly by the year 2010, although the absolute amount of irrigated land should increase by 50% or more. The FAO estimates that the total feasible potential for irrigation in Africa is only 20-25 million ha, or 3-4% of all potentially arable land. These are areas where both rainfall is inadequate and water resources for irrigation are available.[61] Nevertheless, the potential contribution of improved and expanded irrigation is high.

Figure 7a. Estimated, projected, and total potential arable land in the developing world (90 countries), 1974-2000. Source: FAO, 1981.

Rainfed agriculture

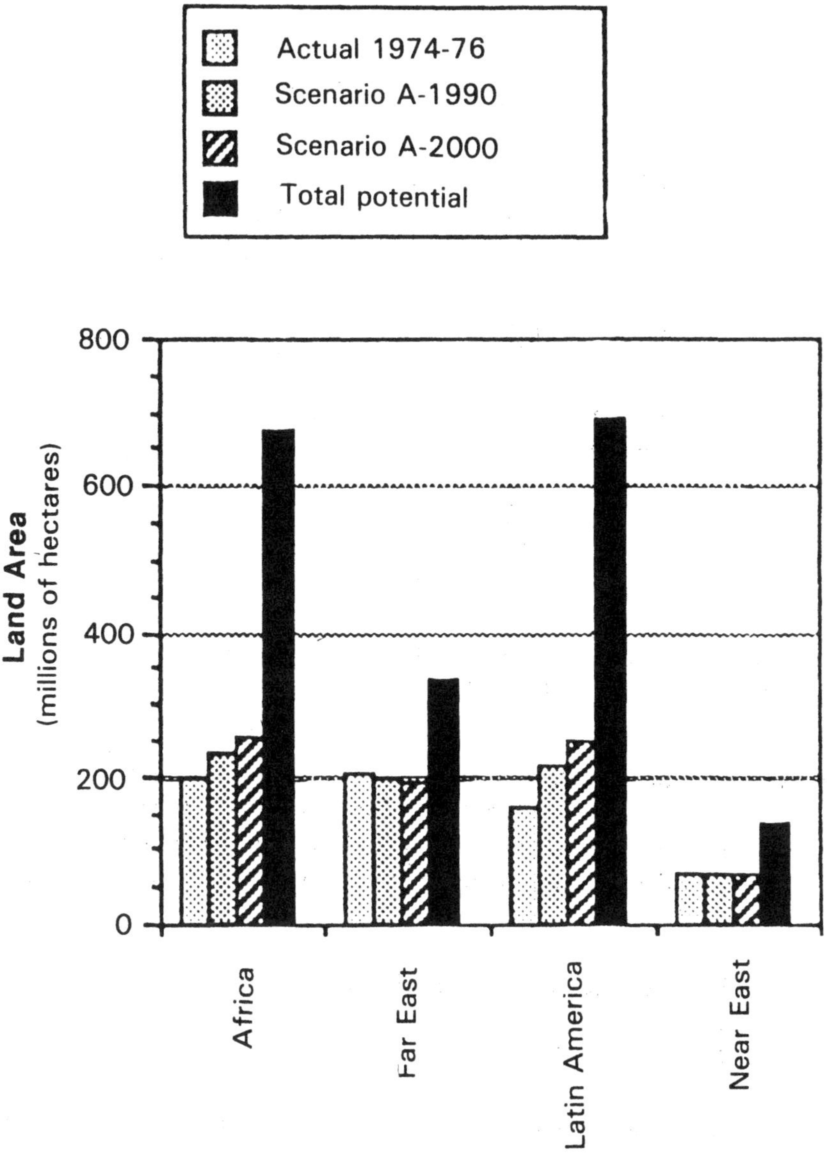

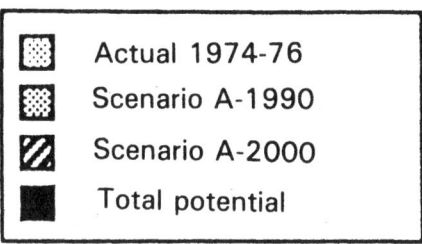

58 BEYOND HUNGER IN AFRICA

Figure 7b. Estimated, projected, and total potential arable land in the developing world (90 countries), 1974 – 2000. Source: FAO, 1981.

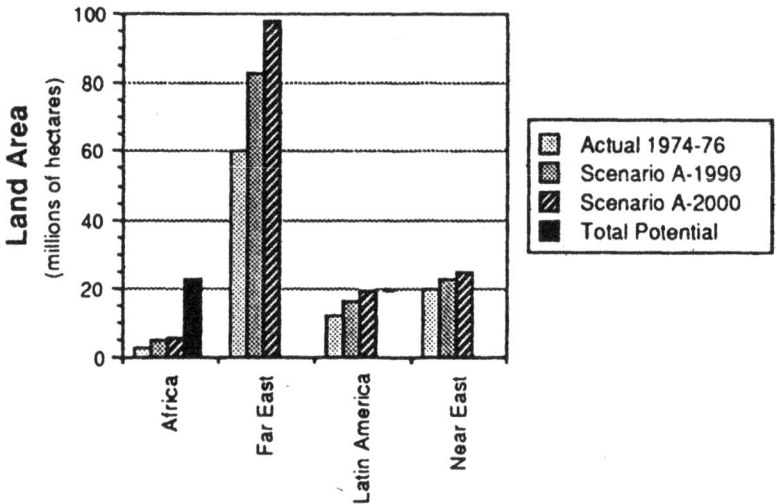

Irrigated agriculture*

*Total potential irrigated area not available for other regions. African value of 20 – 25 million ha is for all of Africa (FAO, 1986).

The FAO projects that irrigated land will account for some 12% of total cereal production in sub-Saharan Africa and 18% in Africa as a whole in 2010. Irrigated production is projected to provide up to one-fifth of Africa's total potential population-supporting capacity in 2000 at low levels of input.[62]

6. Human Resource Trends

6.1 Education and Literacy

Impressive gains have been made in education and literacy in the past two decades. Between 1960 and 1980, the number of children enrolled in school grew by a factor of 3.5 among those 6-11 years old, a lactor of 4 among those 12-17 years old, and a factor of 7 among those 18-23 years old. By 1980, almost two-thirds of the 6-11 year age group and over one-third of the 12-17 year age group, a total of about 75 million children, were enrolled in primary and secondary school. Adult literacy rates have almost tripled since 1960 to about 43% of the sub-Saharan population. The number of universities in sub-Saharan Africa has grown from 6 in 1960 to 57 at present.[63]

Although progress has been encouraging, large gaps remain between present educational levels in Africa and those in the developed world. Some 70 million African children between the ages of 6 and 17 do not attend school. Among those who do, 1 in 10 are estimated to drop out before grade 2, and 2 in 10 before grade 4.[64] Enrolment ratios vary greatly, from as low as 17% in primary school in Niger to 98% in Tanzania.[65] Female enrolment lags significantly behind male enrolment, especially at higher levels of education. Similarly, females constitute about 60% of the illiterate population, a proportion that is expected to persist for the next two decades.[66]

If present trends in school enrolment continue, the UN Educational, Scientific and Cultural Organization (UNESCO) projects that 80% of the 6-11 year age group and 50% of the 12-17 age group would be in school in the year 2000.[67] Since the number of children in these age groups will also rise substantially, nearly doubling from 1980 to 2000, annual growth of more than 4% in primary-school enrolment and over 5% in secondary-school enrolment would be necessary. Despite such rapid growth, the number of children aged 6-17 not in school would still rise by 20%, to 85 million. The school-age population is not expected to level off in Africa until after 2030.

Increased enrolments imply increasing numbers of teachers and increasing expenditures on education. In 1983, there were some 1.6 million teachers in sub-Saharan Africa. Expenditures on education amounted to about $6,200 million (1983 US dollars), 3.5% of total GNP (and about the same as military expenditures).[68] Maintenance of present pupil-teacher ratios and per-pupil expenditures in the future will require comparable growth in the number of teachers and in educational outlays. For example, in the ECA's normative scenario, it is estimated that 4 million teachers would be needed by 2008 for a pupil-teacher ratio of 40.[69]

6.2 Scientific and Technological Capacity

Technological change clearly can make important contributions to future economic growth, increased agricultural and industrial productivity, and improved living standards. Unfortunately, data on indigenous scientific and technological capacity are extremely limited and of poor quality, making it difficult to assess its role in long-term economic development. In part, this is due to the sheer complexity of measuring scientific and technological progress, but it also stems from the scarcity of resources for planning and managing research activities in most of Africa.

Possible indicators of scientific and technological capacity include measures of inputs such as research and development funding or scientific and technical employment and measures of outputs such as the number of patents or the rate of publication. UNESCO has attempted to tabulate data on selected 'input' variables for every country, including the numbers of scientists, engineers, and technicians per million inhabitants and annual expenditures for research and development. However, few African countries report any data at all, and what data there are often have many definitional inconsistencies and other problems. In many instances, data on higher education are used in lieu of more specific information. In those countries with data, reported personnel and expenditure levels are an order of magnitude or more lower than those in developed countries.[70]

Some crude estimates of the worldwide distribution of scientists and engineers engaged in research and development (R&D) and associated expenditures do exist. One UNIDO report describes preliminary results of 1978 World R&D Survey, in which there were on the order of 28,000 researchers (scientists and engineers in R&D) in Africa (excluding South Africa) in 1973, equivalent to 1.2% of the world total and about 68 per million inhabitants.[71] A more recent UNESCO-sponsored report gives a much lower figure for Africa (excluding Arab states) in 1978: only 15,000 scientists and engineers in R&D, or 0.7% of the world total and 53 per million inhabitants.[72] R&D expenditures range from $300 million in 1973 in the first report to $500 million in 1978 in the second report. Africa, Asia, and South and Central Africa all spent less than 0.4% of their GNP on R&D in 1973 and less than 0.5% in 1978.

The above estimate of the number of Africa researchers undoubtedly overstate the number of those active in R&D. Perhaps a more accurate indicator of the latter is the number of African scientists and engineers who publish in scientific journals. One study of almost 4,000 journals, including 85 from developing countries, identified some 4,200 authors from 35 African countries in 1976. In 1971, only about 2,200 authors had been found, suggesting a rather high growth rate of 14% per year over the 6-year period. Growth appears to have slowed in 1975-79, to only about 4% per year in sub-Saharan Africa. Authors were highly concentrated, with most from South Africa, Egypt, and Nigeria. The mean number of authors per million inhabitants was 11 in 1975, and only 7 if South Africa is excluded. Two-thirds of the scientific authors were in the university sector, one-sixth in the public sector, and one-eighth in various UN and other international organizations. Some 60% of the articles published in 1975 were in biology and medicine, 30% in agricultural and environmental sciences, and the remainder in the physical sciences.[73]

It does not appear that any specific projections of the scientific and technical work force have been made. Nevertheless, it is certain that demand for trained scientists, engineers, and managers will grow substantially. In the ECA's normative scenario, for example, it is estimated that some 8,000 engineers and chemists, 65,000 managers and supervisors, and 28,000 skilled workers and foremen would be required by 2008 to expand fertilizer production to meet domestic demand. Expansion of the iron and steel industry implies a need for 19,000 engineers and managers and 33,000 technical personnel.[74] How large the gap will be between the supply of suitably trained Africans and the demand for their services is an important but unanswered question.

7. Natural Resource and Environmental Trends

Africa's many natural resources and diverse environments are a rich endowment. The continent has huge fossil fuel reserves, large mineral supplies, varied ecological and agricultural resources, and considerable potential for hydroelectric, solar, and wind power generation. These have been, and will continue to be, important ingredients in Africa's economic development.

In turn, the pace and direction of economic development in Africa will greatly affect the quality and productivity of its natural resources base and environment. Many adverse effects of development — e.g., accelerated soil erosion, deforestation, and desertification—have already become part of the current gloomy perspective on Africa's future. Other aspects—e.g. impacts on air and water quality, the potential for ecological restoration and protection, and the long-run potential for alternative energy sources—have received relatively little attention.

7.1 Energy

7.1.1 Non-Renewable Energy Resources and Production

Africa is moderately well endowed with mineral energy resources. It has the fourth largest reserves of oil and natural gas. Its proved coal reserves, although only about 2% of world total, are likely to be sufficient for at least 90 years even with a 2.6% per year growth in gross production.[75] It may have between 15-30% of world uranium resources.[76]

Much of Africa has not been thoroughly explored for potential fossil-fuel resources. Areas where further significant oil discoveries are possible include Algeria, Tunisia, Chad, the Niger delta, Zaire, Somalia, and the Rift Valley. In South Africa, estimates of resources increased by 30% and reserves by 60% between the 1978 World Energy Conference Survey and the 1980 World Coal Study. Botswana's reserves may be 10 times higher than indicated in official statistics.[77]

Overall energy production in sub-Saharan Africa grew almost 15% per year in the 1960-74 period. In 1974-81, the average growth rate slowed dramatically, to only 5.6% per year. Indeed, in Africa as a whole, total primary energy production actually declined 15% between 1980 and 1983.[78] Energy production is generally expected to have revived with restoration of positive economic growth rates in Africa in the mid-1980s.

Total oil production is not likely to increase greatly by the end of the century. In the ECA historical-trend scenario, crude oil production increases an average of 1.9% per year between 1978 and 2008. Indeed, production could actually decline due to the finite lifetime of known oil reserves. For example, Nigeria's proved reserves will last only 18 years at 1983 production levels. If probable reserves are included, the lifetime increases to 33 years. Algeria's reserves would last 39 years and Libya's

68 years at 1983 production levels. For Africa, as a whole, proved oil reserves would last 34 years, and proved and probable reserves, 61 years.[79]

Natural gas production has grown rapidly since the 1970s and is expected to continue to grow during the next few decades. Between 1972 and 1980, Algeria's production increased more than eightfold, principally due to its expanded export of natural gas in liquefied form (LNG). Since 1980, its production has declined, but this has been more than counterbalanced by large increases in production in Libya and Nigeria. By the year 2000, Algeria's net export potential could increase by a factor of 8-13 over 1980 levels. A comparable increase is expected for Nigeria. In the ECA historical trends scenario, overall natural gas production increases 5.6% per year during 1978-2008.[80]

Africa produces 4-5% of the world's coal. In 1980-83, South Africa's production grew about 6% per year, much faster than the worldwide growth rate of 1%. The small amount of coal production outside of South Africa declined more than 3% per year during this period. About onefifth of South Africa's production was exported in 1982. These exports constituted 13% of total world trade in coal in that year. South Africa could also have the capacity to produce 10 million metric tons of synthetic liquid fuels from coal by the year 2000.[81]

Continued growth in coal production is expected through the year 2000, averaging 5.5% per year. Growth in exports could average 2.7% per year. Production growth outside of South Africa is likely to be slower. For example, in the ECA's historical scenario, total production increases only 2.5% per year between 1978 and 2008 in ECA countries.[82]

7.1.2 Renewable Energy Resources and Production

Africa's hydroelectric power potential is larger than that of any other major world region. However, present installed energy capacity is only about 1-2% of the total potential recoverable resource. This is partly due to the relatively high capital cost of hydroelectric facilities, 50% or more than oil-fired power plants on average, and their often lengthy construction times. An added problem is that much of the potential capacity is located far from population and industrial centres.[83]

Nevertheless, hydroelectric power already plays an important role in Africa's energy balance, contributing 9-10% to present energy consumption and 25-30% to total electric production. In 18 countries, it comprised more than half of installed electrical capacity in 1983. Hydroelectric capacity increased by an average of 9.6% per year in 1968-78, but slowed to 4.6% in 1980-83. The ECA projects that capacity will increase 7.5% per year in ECA countries through 2008. Maintaining this growth rate will certainly require large annual investments.[84]

Geothermal resources are another virtually untapped energy resource. By one estimate, Africa's geothermal electric potential is two-fifths of its hydroelectric potential. Only Kenya has any significant installed capacity. Its geothermal production in 1983 was equal to 12% of its total electricity production.[85]

Africa has vast solar and wind resources. Total solar installation is second only to the Middle East. Most coastal areas have mean annual wind speeds of 7m/s or more. Unfortunately, utilization of these resources for power generation has been very limited. Present technologies have high capital costs and require sophisticated technological inputs. In the medium- to long-term, photovoltaic power generation is very promising, and is already economical in some specialized applications. Costs could drop significantly over the next few decades, especially if more cost-effect energy storage methods can be devised.[86]

About 45% of Africa's land area is covered with forests, forest regrowth, or woody vegetation. Utilization of this extensive resource generates a significant portion of total energy production from all energy sources on the continent. In 1983, for example, Africa's total commercial energy production was 497 million metric tons of coal equivalent (TCE). Total fuelwood production was 421 million cubic metres, equivalent to 147 million TCE. Production of fuelwood and charcoal increased 4.5% per year between 1951 and 1975 in sub-Saharan Africa (excluding South Africa) and 3% per year between 1973 and 1983 in Africa as a whole.[87]

Although overall supplies of wood greatly exceed demand in Africa as a whole, imbalances already exist at the regional level (Figure 8). Demand in North Africa greatly exceeds supply. In East Africa, demand is one-third larger than supply. By 2010, deficits are projected to have developed in the Sudano-Sahelian region and western and southern Africa. Africa as a whole will continue to have a net surplus, simply because central Africa's supply is so large. Reforestation efforts are expanding, but they still fall far short of the level needed to maintain sus-

Figure 8: Estimated and projected fuelwood supply and demand by agro-ecological region of Africa, 1980-2010. Source: FAO, 1986d.

(a) 1980

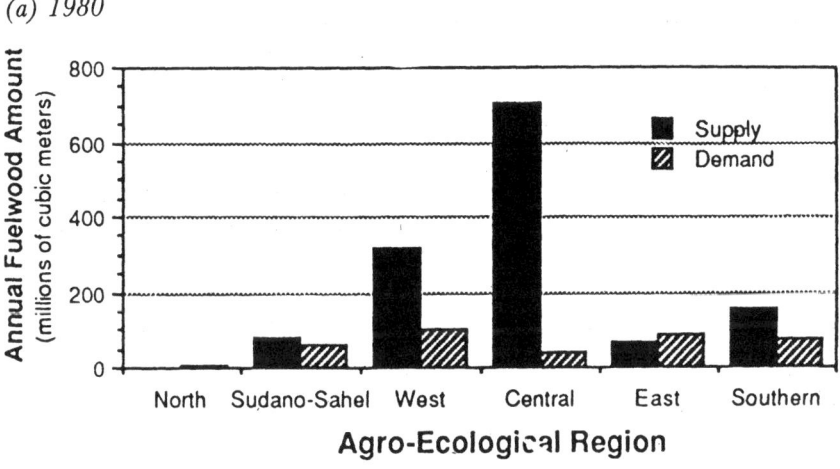

(b) 2010

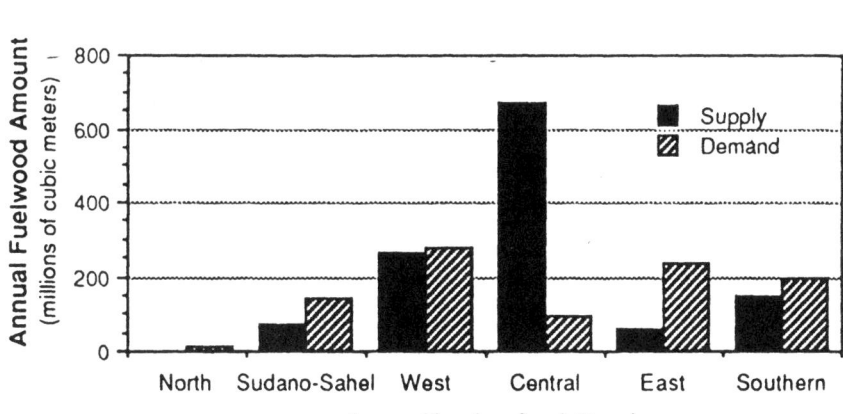

tainable yields. For example, it has been estimated that planting rates would have to increase by factors of 5 to 50 in 9 African countries in order to meet domestic fuelwood requirements through the year 2000.[88]

Other renewable energy resources such as biomass production and utilization of urban waste also have considerable potential within Africa. Potential biomass availability in Africa could be as high as 3,000 million metric tons from agricultural waste and 47,000 million metric tons from energy farms.[89] These estimates are probably optimistic for Africa since they are based on rates of agricultural and urban waste found in the US and since biomass production on energy farms is likely to be limited severely by land, fertilizer, and capital constraints.[90]

On the other hand, technologies such as biogas production have been successfully and rapidly introduced elsewhere in the developing world. China introduced small-scale biogas digesters in 1970-72, and by 1977 had over 4 million units serving tens of millions of people.[91] In Africa, the potential for biogas production is also large. A major resource is the 160 million head of cattle that the FAO estimates existed in Africa in 1983. Each year, these animals produce on the order of 900 million tons of dung with an energy content equivalent to 100 million tons of coal.[92] Some fast-growing tree species could also provide sustainable yields of 30 TCE per hectare with a four to five year harvesting cycle. If 20% of Africa's forested area were replaced with these species, per capita production could in principle exceed 5 TCE per person, more than ten times current energy consumption in sub-Saharan Africa.[93]

7.1.3 Energy Consumption

Per capita consumption of energy has more than doubled in the past two decades in sub-Saharan Africa, but is still lower than consumption in most other developing areas. Growth rates were 10.6% per year in 1960-74 and 3.6% per year in 1974-81.[94] Per capita consumption varies greatly between countries (Figure 9). Only 12 countries with one-fourth of Africa's population had per capita consumption at or above Africa's mean of 0.42 TCE per person. Only 16 countries with 30% of the population had per capita consumption greater than one-half of the mean. In other words, over 300 million Africans live in areas where per capita energy consumption was 0.2 TCE or less. Mean per capita consumption in North America and Europe is 20-30 times higher.

Consumption of commercial energy is evenly split between solid and liquid fuels, each with two-fifths of total consumption. The remaining consumption is met with natural gas (12%) and electricity (3%). However, these aggregate figures conceal the much higher dependence

Figure 9. Energy consumption per capita for countries and territories of Africa, 1983. Source: UN, 1983c.

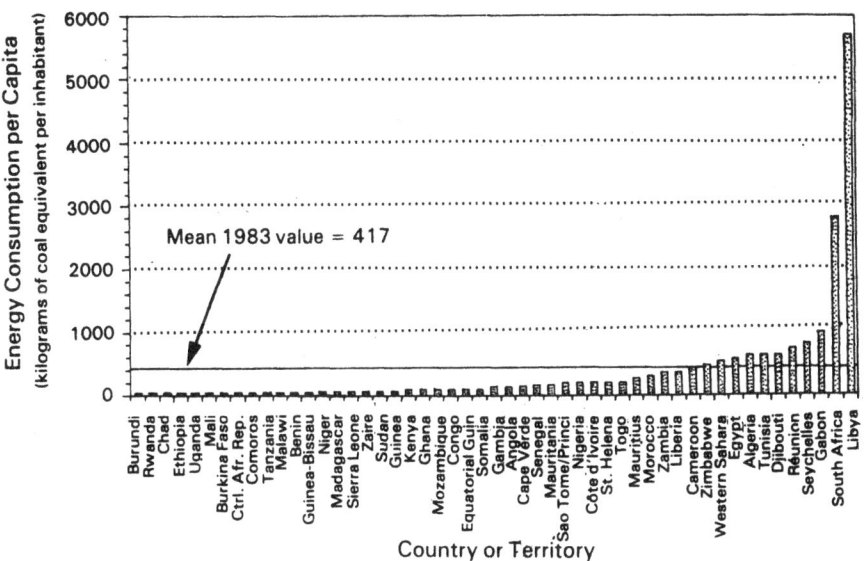

of most African countries on oil. In particular, 40 of 51 African countries and territories containing 60% of the continent's population relied on oil for more than three-fourths of their commercial energy consumption in 1983. Of these, 25 imported most or all of their oil.[95]

Agriculture's share of commercial energy consumption is small. In the developing market economies of Africa, it consumed only 5.4% in 1982. About half of this energy was used for fertilizer manufacture, packaging, transport, and distribution. Farm machinery consumed the next largest amount, 41% in 1982. Pumped irrigation claimed only 4.5%, and pesticide used a small but growing share (1.5% in 1972 and 5.5% in 1982). Between 1972 and 1982, energy use per agricultural worker increased by 30% in developing Africa, and energy use per hectare of arable land increased by 13%.[96] These levels of energy use were the lowest of any developing region.

Energy consumption in other sectors is much larger. For developing Africa and South and Southeast Asia taken together, transportation consumed 30% of final energy demand in 1975, buildings in the household and service sectors consumed 10%, and agriculture, manufacturing, mining, and construction consumed the remaining 60%. These shares are not expected to change drastically even by 2030, according to one study.[97]

7.1.4 Projections of Energy Supply and Demand

There have been numerous studies of future energy supply and demand in the world as a whole and in developed regions. However, relatively few have dealt specifically with energy issues in the developing world, and even fewer have looked in detail at Africa.[98]

In the interfutures scenarios, energy demand in Africa south of the Sahara was projected to increase by a factor of 3 to 5 between 1975 and 2000. In the low case, north-south confrontation leads to stagnation of world production and trade and therefore to depressed energy consumption in less developed regions. In the high case, increased polarization and protectionism among developed countries inspire greater co-operation and trade between the European Economic Community and Africa, leading to increased energy exports from Africa. Intermediate increases in energy demand are projected for the more conventional moderate and high growth scenarios. The implied growth rate in per capita energy demand is 2-4% per year.[99]

In a major study conducted by the International Institute for Applied Systems Analysis (IIASA), energy demand in a region containing Africa, south Asia, and Southeast Asia increases by a factor of about 3.5 from 1975 to 2000 in a low-growth scenario and by 4.5 in a high-growth scenario. By 2030, demand is 8 times larger than in 1975 in the low scenario and 14.5 times larger in the high scenario. Over 1975-2030, per capital energy consumption increases by 3.5 in the low scenario, or 2.3% per year on average, and by 6.5 in the high scenario, or 3.5% per year. The shares of oil and coal in total primary demand decrease through at least 2025 in both scenarios, while the shares of gas renewables and hydroelectric and nuclear power increase significantly.[100]

A more recent projection by an energy-industry analysis shows African primary energy demand increasing an average of 5.1% per year between 1983 and 2000. Oil demand increases only 3.1% per year, and hydroelectricity at 2% per year, so that their contribution to total de-

PROJECTING THE CURRENT PERSPECTIVE 69

mand decreases substantially by 2000. Demand for coal and gas, on the other hand, increases at 6.0% and 10.1% per year, respectively. Assuming a 3.0% per year growth in the African population over the same period, overall per capita energy consumption is estimated to grow 2.2% per year.[101]

Long-range energy projections developed by Edmonds and Reilly indicate that energy consumption would increase by a factor of 22 between 1975 and 2050 in Africa, implying an average growth rate of 4.2%. This compares with a projected growth rate of 2.5% for the world as a whole. In their model, the population of Africa increases only 1.4% per year, a much lower growth rate than that implied by the standard World Bank projection. The low figure yields a growth rate in per capita energy consumption of 2.8% per year. A higher figure derived from the World Bank standard projection (2% per year over 1980-2055) yields a growth rate of 2.2% per year.[102]

7.2 Environmental Trends

A major source of pessimism about Africa's future has been concern over accelerating environmental degradation and the long-term sustainability of agricultural development. Africa's physical environment is fragile. Much of its soil is weak in nutrients and incapable of sustaining intensified uses without costly fertilizer and machinery inputs. In many areas, soil erosion threatens both agricultural productivity and hydroelectric power generation. Rainfall is highly variable, and surface water supplies in many cases are limited and vulnerable to pollution.

The FAO estimates that as much as 12% of the tropical forest in the developing world will be cleared between 1980 and 2000. About half of this is for shifting cultivation, which would generally permit forest regrowth after cropping. High rates of deforestation are reported in a number of African countries. Ethiopia's forests may have decreased by some three-fourths in area from the 1950s to 1970s. Satellite imagery of one section of Kenya shows significant decreases in forest cover between 1973 and 1978. Côte d'Ivoire has the highest reported deforestation rate, with nearly a 10% per year decrease in closed forest area on average in 1981-5. Apparently, some of the cleared land is being planted with tree crops, thereby compensating to some degree for the loss of wood resources.[103] Nevertheless, uncontrolled deforestation is a serious concern. Its consequences extend beyond diminished fuelwood supplies to adverse impacts on soil erosion and siltation, flood control, moisture storage, biological diversity, and other forest-based resources.

Degradation of soils through erosion, crusting, leaching, and other processes is another major environmental problem in Africa. Sheet erosion affects 34 countries moderately and another 15 slightly, according to the FAO. Wind erosion is a moderate to severe problem in most of northern and Sahelian Africa. Encroachment by the desert and crusting of the upper soil layers are prevalent throughout the Sahel and to a lesser extent in other parts of Africa. Moderate declines in soil fertility due to leaching of nutrients and reduced fallow periods appear to be a problem in most of sub-Saharan Africa.[104]

One of soil erosion's most damaging consequences is its impact on water resources. Siltation of dams and hydroelectric facilities can be very costly. For example, it is reported that siltation may have cut the useful life of some of Kenya's dams in half.[105] Heavy sediment loads can also damage fisheries, create navigational problems, and reduce recreational and tourism values.

Desertification poses a third major threat to Africa's environment. More than one-fifth of the continent is desert and one-tenth has sandy soil. Another 50% may be susceptible to desertification if not properly managed. Specific problems associated with desertification include drifting sand and dust, severe surface erosion, salinization of soils, reduced groundwater recharge, disruption of wildlife, and modification of plant species leading to lower primary production.[106]

Livestock, and the tendency to overgraze them, are a major contributor to desertification. Cattle in particular are poorly suited to Africa's extensive rangelands, since they tend to consume grasses completely, trample seedlings, compact soil, and require large amounts of water. Nevertheless, cattle populations have grown dramatically, even at the expense of other more adaptive and less environmentally damaging livestock types. If such growth continues, areas at risk of desertification could expand greatly.[107]

Deforestation, soil erosion, and desertification are the most often cited threats to the environment of Africa, but they are not the only ones. Air pollution, acid deposition, groundwater depletion, pesticide and heavy-metal contamination, environmental diseases, and climatic change are some of the many possible environmental problems that could significantly influence Africa's long-term future. However, these do not generally enter into the "current perspective" on Africa's future, in part because they tend to be viewed as too uncertain or too distant. But, if many of the economic and social changes detailed in this scenario (or others) do come about over the next 80 years—for example, rapid growth in fossil-fuel consumption and in use of fertilizers and pesticides —some of these environmental problems could emerge as critical. If they do, they would probably have important feedbacks into economic, social, or even demographic development in Africa.

Figure 10: Population density by country of Africa, 1985-2055, World Bank standard projection. Countries are ranked by their densities in 1985. Source: VU, 1985.

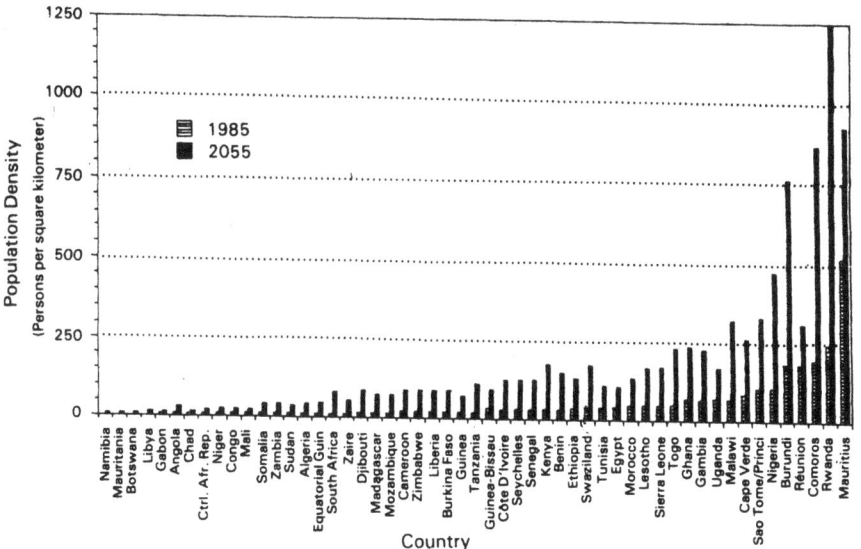

In this connection, it is useful to conclude this discussion with a look at the population densities that could exist in Africa's future in 2055 (Figure 10). Clearly, there could be a number of countries with densities higher than those which exist in Indonesia and Bangladesh today.[108] The implicit resource demands and environmental stresses are unprecedented, but, in the context of seventy years of development, might not be overwhelming. Of perhaps more importance is that the variation in population density appears to be greater. Some countries would still have lower densities than the majority of countries today. By inference, there may be considerably greater variation in the level of resource use and environmental stress. Africa could begin to experience the added difficulties of transboundary pollution, resource competition, exportation of problems and so forth that the developed world is experiencing today.

NOTES:

1. Interfutures Project, 1979.
2. More detailed background data and discussion may be found in Chen, 1987.
3. UN General Assembly, 1986, pp.4-5; World Bank, 1986b, p.1; Committee on African Development Strategies, 1985.
4. World Bank, 1986c, pp.39-40.
5. ECA, 1986, p.60; World Bank, 1986a, p.214; Green and Griffith-Jones, 1986, pp.22-26.
6. World Bank, 1986a, p.186; ECA, 1986, pp.18-24.
7. ECA, 1986, p.29; World Resources Institute (WRI), 1986, p.266.
8. WRI, 1986, p.270-278.
9. Vu, 1985, p.9.
10. Based on distribution of GNP in 1983 reported by the Population Reference Bureau, 1986.
11. Based on data for 2055 from Vu, 1985.
12. Sub-Saharan Africa includes all African countries except Algeria, Egypt, Libyan Arab Jamahiriya, Morocco, Sudan, Tunisia, and Western Sahara.
13. UN, 1986, pp.23-27.
14. Vu, 1985; UN Secretariat, 1983a, p.25 (long-range UN projections, medium variant, as assessed in 1980).
15. For example, both projections assume that migration flows decrease to zero in the next few decades (see Chen, 1987).
16. UN, 1985a p.1; UN, 1973, 1986a; see Chen, 1987.
17. UN, 1985b, p.44.
18. World Bank, 1986b, p.27; World Bank, 1986d, pp.35-36.
19. UN, 1985a, Vu, 1985, p.xiv.
20. UN, 1986, p.38; UN 1985b. 132.
21. UN, 1986, p.143.
22. Vu, 1985, p.8-9.
23. UN, 1983b.
24. The UN estimates, part of a special study, are up to 10 per cent higher than those in the 1984 UN population projections, presumably due to different assumptions about life expectancy and age-specific mortality (UN Secretariat, 1983b). Estimates by the US Bureau of Census (1986) for several African countries also differ substantially.
25. US National Reserarch Council, 1983, p.41.
26. UN, 1986.
27. UN, 1985b, pp.197-198; Salas, 1986.
28. World Bank, 1986a, p.55.
29. This is true even if GDP data are adjusted for the bias due to the use of exchange rates (McGreevey, 1985).
30. World Bank, 1984a, pp.34, 35, 37.
31. Hodd, 1986, based on World Bank projections.
32. World Bank, 1986a, p.48.
33. ECA, p.50; UNIDO, 1983, pp.42-45.

34. ECA, 1983, p.50; UNIDO, 1983, pp.42-45.
35. Interfutures Project, 1979. Population growth projections are adapted from UN and OECD estimates.
36. World Bank, 1983a.
37. UNIDO, 1983, p.101; World Bank, 1984b, p.58.
38. Over half of Africa's 1979 MVA was due to Algeria, Egypt, Morocco, and Nigeria (UNIDO, 1983, p.106).
39. UNIDO, 1983, 1985.
40. UNIDO, 1985, p.77.
41. The corresponding GDP growth rate is 6.2% (UNIDO, 1983, p.42).
42. UNIDO, 1983, p.30, 44.
43. Interfutures Project, 1979, pp.330-331.
44. World Bank, 1986a, p.3. See Chen, 1987, for a discussion of agricultural employment.
45. World Bank, 1984b, p.77; ECA, 1986; World Bank, 1983a.
46. FAO, 1986b, e; US Department of Agriculture, 1986, 1987.
47. World Bank, 1984b, pp.77-79; World Bank, 1983b.
48. Based on a deficiency level of 80% of the FAO/WHO requirement (World Bank, 1986c, p.18).
49. CEQ 1980, p.94; FAO, 1981, p.21; FAO, 1986c, p.9; Islam, 1982.
50. FAO, 1986c, pp.20-23; Sarma, 1986, p.44; Paulino, 1986, p.71. Also see Chen, 1987.
51. Paulino, 1986, p.22; Paulino, 1987, pp.28-30.
52. CEQ, 1980, p.559, footnote b to Table 18-12.
53. Linneman et al., 1979, p.247; FAO, 1980, Tables A-1 and A-2 (excludes South Africa); FAO, 1981, Statistical Annex Table 3; FAO, 1986c, p.16.
54. FAO, 1981, p.133.
55. e.g. CEQ, 1980; FAO, 1981, 1986c. See Chen, 1987, for a more detailed discussion.
56. Islam, 1982, pp.28-35.
57. Paulino, 1987, p.30; FAO, 1984, p.43.
58. Islam, 1982, p.31. In Scenario B, the average growth rate drops below 0.7% per year over 2000-2030.
59. FAO, 1981, p.66; Islam, 1982, p.31; FAO, 1986d.
60. e.g. Egypt, the Sudan and Madagascar, Grigg, 1985, p.159; FAO, 1986a, p.173; FAO, 1986c, p.17.
61. FAO, 1981, p.67; FAO, 1986c, pp.13-17; FAO, 1986d, p.53.
62. Higgins et al., 1982, p.27. Its contribution is less than 5% at high levels of input.
63. UNESCO, 1984, pp.468-472 (excludes Namibia); World Bank, 1983b; Hinchliffe, 1985, p.9.
64. UNESCO, 1984, 472-482. Based on 35 countries for which data were available.
65. Hinchliffe, 1985, p.7.
66. UNESCO, 1984.
67. UNESCO, 1984, pp.471-474. The ECA's 1983 projections give slightly the higher enrolment ratios.
68. Sivard, 1986, p.35. Over 4% of GNP is spent on education in Africa as a whole (cf., Hinchliffe, 1985, p.80).
69. ECA, 1983, pp.59-60. Compared with 22 or less in developed countries (UNESCO, 1984, p.484).
70. Morita-Lou, 1985, pp.17-19; UNESCO, 1985; France, 1980. Data are summarized in Chen, 1987.
71. UNIDO, 1979, p.181.
72. Clarke, 1985, p.168. The discrepancy between the two reports is presumably due to the large concentration of scientists and engineers in "Arab" countries.
73. Bickenstaff and Maravcsik, 1982; Davis, 1983, pp.166-7.
74. ECA, 1983, pp.74-75.
75. This growth rate is lower than what is generally expected. Edmonds and Reilly, 1985, p.157 (1980 data). Matveev et al.. 1984, p.22, report 1982 data.

76. International Energy Agency (IEA), 1982; Edmonds and Reilly, 1985, p.173, Hedley, 1986, pp.73-75.
77. Dunkerley et al., 1981, pp.138, 141; IEA, 1982, pp.287-288.
78. It dropped 20% in Africa excluding South Africa. World Bank, 1984b, p.62; UN, 1985c, pp.1-8.
79. ECA, 1983, p.34; IEA, 1982; Hedley, 1986, pp.208-209.
80. Hedley, 1986, p.203; IEA, 1982, p.400; ECA, 1983, p.34.
81. Hedley, 1986, pp.163, 192; UN, 1985c, pp.113-114.
82. Hedley, 1986, p.194; ECA, 1983, p.34.
83. Edmonds and Reilly, 1985, pp.219-224; Dunkerley et al., 1986, pp.159-163.
84. ECA, 1983, pp.32-34; UN, 1985c, pp.334-40.
85. Revelle, 1982, p.74; UN, 1985c, pp.336-392.
86. Hayes, 1981, pp.41-42; Edmonds and Reilly, 1985, pp.194-205; Howe et al., 1980.
87. WRI, 1986; IIASA, 1981, p.476; WRI, 1986, p.69.
88. FAO, 1986d, pp.50-51; Hoffman and Johnson, 1981, p.138.
89. e.g., Edmonds and Reilly, 1985, based in part on estimates for the US from the US Department of Energy.
90. e.g., Dunkerley et al., 1984, pp.179-180.
91. Hayes, 1981, p.44; US National Research Council, 1984, pp.17-18.
92. Cattle population from FAO, 1986d, p.31; conversion factors from Makhijani, 1975, p.108 and Chatterji, 1981, p.18.
93. Revelle, 1982, pp.73-74.
94. World Bank, 1983b; World Bank 1984b, p.62.
95. UN, 1985c, Tables 1 and 24.
96. FAO, 1986b, pp.66, 70-71; FAO, 1986c.
97. IIASA, 1981, p.487.
98. For example, the 1980 CEQ study provided forecasts only for less developed countries as a group and the 1981 IIASA study combined sub-Saharan Africa with South and Southeast Asia. For summaries of a number of other studies, see Howe et al., (1980) and Edmonds and Reilly (1985).
99. Interfutures Project, 1979, pp.293-329. Sub-Saharan Africa's population is assumed to grow 2.4% per year over 1975-2000 in the study.
100. IIASA, 1981, pp.682-683, 775. GDP growth rates over 1975-2030 average 3.3% and 4.3% respectively for the low and high scenarios.
101. Hedley, 1986, p.277.
102. Edmonds and Reilly, 1985, pp.25, 282. World Bank data from Vu, 1985.
103. FAO, 1981, pp.80-81; WRI, 1986, p.71; Clark University, 1984, p.45; FAO, 1986d, p.50.
104. FAO, 1986d, p.56.
105. Clark University, 1984, p.76.
106. FAO, 1986d, pp.56-57; US National Research Council, 1983, pp.36-37.
107 US National Research Council, 1983, pp.32-37.
108. Tabah, 1982.

BIBLIOGRAPHY

Blickenstaff, J., and M.J. Moravcsik, 1982. "Scientific output in the Third World", *Scientometrics* 4(2): 135-69.

Brumby, P.J. 1985. "The International Livestock Centre for Africa: Its objectives, activities, and future", *Food for the Future*, The Philadelphia Society for Promoting Agriculture, Philadelphia, pp.102-123.

Chen, R.S. 1987. "Africa's future: The current perspective, 1957-2057", Research Report RR-97-1, Alan Shawn Feinstein World Hunger Program, Brown University, Providence, RI.

Clark University, 1984. *Renewable Resource Trends in East Africa*, Program for International Development, Clark University, Worcester, MA.

Clarke, R., 1985. *Science and Technology in World Development* (New York: Oxford University/UNESCO).

Committee on African Development Strategies, 1985. *Compact for African Development: Report of the Committee on African Development Strategies*, Council of Foreign Relations, New York, and Overseas Development Council, Washington, DC.
Council on Environmental Quality, 1980. *The Global 2000 Report to The President: Entering the Twenty-First Century, Volume II, Technical Report*, U.S. Government Printing Office, Washington, DC.
Davis, C.H., 1983. "Institutional sectors of 'mainstream' science production in sub-Saharan Africa, 1970-1979: A quantitative analysis", *Scientometrics* 5(3): 163-175.
Dunkerley, J., W. Rsay, L. Gordon, and E. Cecelski, 1981. *Energy Strategies for Development Nations* (Baltimore: Johns Hopkins University).
Economic Commission for Africa, 1983. *ECA and Africa's Development 1983-2008: A Preliminary Perspective Study*, United Nations Economic Commission for Africa, Addis Ababa.
Economic Commission for Africa, 1986. *African Socio-Economic Indicators 1984*, United Nations Economic Commission for Africa, Addis Ababa.
Edmonds, J., and J.M. Reilly, 1985. *Global Energy: Assessing the Future* (New York: Oxford University).
Food and Agriculture Organization, 1980. *Regional Food Plan for Africa*, Food and Agriculture Organization of the United Nations, Rome.
Food and Agriculture Organization, 1981. *Agriculture: Toward 2000*, Economic and Social Development Series 23, Food and Agriculture Organization of the United Nations, Rome.
Food and Agriculture Organization, 1984. *Land, Food and People*, Food and Agriculture, Organization of the United Nations, Rome.
Food and Agriculture Organization, 1986a. The State of Food and Agriculture 1985: Mid-Decade Review of Food and Agriculture, *FAO Agriculture Series* 19, Food and Agriculture Organization of the United Nations, Rome.
Food and Agriculture Organization, 1986b. *The State of Food and Agriculture 1986*, Council, Ninetieth Session, CL 90/2, Food and Agriculture Organization of the United Nations, Rome.
Food and Agriculture Organization, 1986c. *African Agriculture: The Next 25 Years, Main Report*, Food and Agriculture Organization of the United Nations, Rome.
Food and Agriculture Organization, 1986d. *African Agriculture: The Next 25 Years, Atlas of African Agriculture*, Food and Agriculture Organization of the United Nations, Rome.
Food and Agriculture Organization, 1986e. Foodcrops and Shortages, Special Report 11 (November).
Food and Agriculture Organization, 1986f. *World Agricultural Statistics: FAO Statistical Pocketbook*, Food and Agriculture Organization of the United Nations, Rome.
Frame, J.D., 1980. "Measuring scientific activity in lesser developed countries", *Scientometrics* 2 (2): 135-145.
Green, R.H., and S. Griffith-Jones, 1986. "Sub-Saharan Africa's external debt crises", *Third World Affairs 1986*, R. Gauhar, Ed. (Boulder, Co: Westview), pp.17-32.
Grigg, D., 1985. *The World Food Problem 1950-80* (Oxford: Basil Blackwell).
Hayes, D., 1981. "Energy for development: Third World options," *Energy and Environment in the Developing Countries*, M. Chatterji, Ed. (New York: John Wiley).
Hedley, D. 1986. *World Energy: The Facts and the Future*, Second Edition (New York: Facts on File Publications).
Higgins, G.M., A.H. Kassam, L. Naiken, G. Fischer, and M.M. Shah, 1982. *Potential Population Supporting Capacities of Lands in the Developing World*, FPA/INT/513, Food and Agriculture Organization of the United Nations, United Nations Fund for Population Activies, and the International Institute for Applied Systems Analysis, Rome.
Hinchliffe, K., 1985. "Issues related to higher education in sub-Saharan Africa" *World Bank Staff Working Papers* 780, The World Bank, Washington, DC.
Hodd, M., *African Economic Handbook* (London: Euromonitor Publications).
Hoffman, T., and B. Johnson, 1981. The World Energy Triangle: A Strategy for Co-operation (Cambridge, MA: Ballinger).
Howe, J.W., J.J. Tarrant III, and J.A. Martin. 1980. "South-North Co-operation on energy for development," *Energy Futures of Developing Countries: The Neglected Victims of the Energy Crisis*, H. Cleveland, Ed., Aspen Institute for Humanistic Studies, New York, pp.19-78.

Interfutures Project, 1979. Facing the Future: Mastering the Probable and Managing the Unpredictable, Organization for Economic Co-operation and Development, Paris.
International Energy Agency, 1982. *World Energy Outlook*. Organization for Economic Co-operation and Development, Paris.
International Institute for Applied System Analysis, 1981. *Energy in a Finite World: A Global Systems Analysis* (Cambridge, MA: Ballinger).
Islam, N., 1982. "Food", *Population and the World Economy in the 21st Century*, J. Faaland, Ed. (New York: St Martin's), pp.23-49.
Leontief, W., 1980. "Population growth and economic development" *Population Bulletin of the United Nations* 12-1979, United Nations Department of International Economic and Social Affairs, ST/ESA/Ser.N/12, New York, pp.69-82.
Leontief, W., and I. Sohn, 1982. "Economic Growth", *Population and the World Economy in the 21st Century*, J. Faaland, Ed. (New York: St. Martin's), pp.96-127.
Leontief, W., et al., 1977. *The Future of the World Economy* (New York: Oxford University).
Linneman, H., J. De Hoogh, M.A. Keyzer and H.D.J. Van Heemst, 1979. *Moira: Model of International Relations in Agriculture, Contributions to Economic Analysis* 24. (Amsterdam: North Holand).
Makhijani, A., 1975. *Energy and Agriculture in the Third World* (Cambridge, MA: Ballinger).
Matveev, A.K., V.S. Borisov, N.G. Zheleznova, V.R. Kler, Yu.R. Mazor, K.V. Mironov, and V.F. Cherepovaski, 1984. "World Resources of coals", *Energy Resources of the World, Colloquium 2 Reports, Volume 2*, 27th International Geological Congress, Publishing Office, Nauka, Moscow, pp.11-25.
McGreevey, W.P., 1985. "Economic aspects of historical demographic change," *World Bank Staff Working Papers* 685 and *Population and Development Series* 10, The World Bank, Washington, DC.
Morita-Lou, H., 1985 *Science and Technology Indicators for Development* (Boulder, Colorado: Westview).
Pauliino, L.A. 1986. "Food in the Third World: Past trends and projections to 2000", *Research Report* 52, International Food Policy Research Institute, Washington, DC.
Paulino, L.A., 1987. "The evolving food situation", *Accelerating Food Production in Sub-Saharan Africa*, J.W. Mellor, C.L. Delgado, and M.J. Blackie, eds. (Baltimore: Johns Hopkins University), pp.23-28.
Population Reference Bureau, 1986. *1986 World Population Data Sheet*, Population Reference Bureau, Inc., Washington, DC.
Revelle, R. 1982. "Resources", *Population and the World Economy in the 21st Century*, J. Faaland, Ed. (New York: St. Martin's), pp.50-77.
Salas, R.M. 1986. "Population and the urban future", *UNFPA 1985 Report*, United Nations Fund for Population Activities, New York, pp.7-39.
Sarma, J., 1986. "Cereal feed use in the Third World: Past trends and projection to 2000", *Research Report* 57, International Food Policy Research Institute, Washington, DC.
Sivard, R.L., 1986. *World Military and Social Expenditures 1986*, World Priorities, Inc., Washington, DC.
Tabah, L., "Population growth", *Population and the World Economy in the 21st Century*, J. Faaland, Ed. (New York: St. Martin's), pp.175-205.
United Nations, 1973. World Population Prospects: Estimates and Projections as Assessed in 1968, *Population Studies* 53, United Nations Department of Economic and Social Affairs ST/SOA/Ser.A/53, New York.
United Nations, 1985a. World Population Prospects: Estimates and Projections as Assessed in 1982, *Population Studies* 53, United Nations Department of Economic and Social Affairs ST/ESA/Ser.A/86, New York.
United Nations, 1985b. World population trend, Populations and Development Interrelations and Population Policies: 1983 Monitoring Report, Volume I Population Trends, *Population Studies* 93, United Nations Department of International Economic and Social Affairs ST/ESA/Ser.A/93, New York.
United Nations, 1985c. *1983 Energy Statistics Yearbook*, United Nations Department of International Economic and Social Affairs ST/ESA/STAT/Ser.J/27, New York.

United Nations, 1986. World Population Prospects: Estimates and Projections As Assessed in 1984, *Population Studies* 98 United Nations Department of International Economic and Social Affairs ST/ESA/Ser.A/98, New York.

United Nations Educational, Scientific and Cultural Organization, 1984. "Prospects of meeting the education requirements of growing populations", Population, Resources Environment and Development: Procedings of the Expert Group on Population, Resources, Environment and Development, Geneva, 25-29 April 1983, *Population Studies* 90, ST/ESA/Ser.A/90, United Nations, New York, pp. 465-501.

United Nations Educational, Scientific and Cultural Organization, 1985. *UNESCO Statistical Digest 1985: A Statistical Summary of Data on Education, Science and Technology, Culture and Communication, by Country,* United Nations Educational, Scientific and Cultural Organization, Paris.

United Nations General Assembly, 1986. *Report on the Special Session on Africa, May 25-26,* United Nations, New York.

United Nations Industrial Development Organization, 1979. *Industry 2000—New Perspectives,* United Nations, New York.

United Nations Industrial Development Organization, 1983. *Industry in a Changing World: Special Issue of the Industrial Development Survey of the Fourth General Conference of UNIDO,* United Nations, New York.

United Nations Industrial Development Organization, 1985. Industry and Development: Global Report 1985, United Nations, New York.

United Nations Secretariat, 1983a. "Long-range global population projections, as assessed in 1980," *Population Bulletin of the United Nations,* 14-1982, United Nations Department of International Economic and Social Affairs ST/ESA/Ser.N/14, New York, pp.17-30.

United Nations Secretariat, 1983b. "Infant mortality: World estimates and projections, 1950-2025", *Population bulletin of the United Nations* 14-1982, United Nations Department of International Economic and Social Affairs ST/ESA/Ser.N/14, New York, pp.31-53.

U S Bureau of the Census, 1983. *World Population 1983: Recent Demographic Estimates for the Countries and Regions of the World,* US Department of Commerce, Washington, DC.

US Bureau of the Census, 1986. *World Population Profile: 1985,* WP-85, US Department of Commerce, Washington, DC.

US Department of Agriculture, 1986. *World Food Needs and Availabilities, 1986/87,* US Department of Agriculture Economic Research Service, Washington, DC.

US Department of Agriculture, 1987. *World and Needs and Availabilities, 1986/87: Winter Update,* US Department of Agriculture Economic Research Service, Washington, DC.

U.S. National Research Council, 1983, *Environmental Change in the West African Sahel* (Washington, DC: National Academy Press).

US National Research Council, 1984. *Diffusion of Biomas Energy Technologies iin Developing Countries, Second Edition* (Washington, DC. National Academy Press).

US National Research Council, 1986. *Population Growth and Economic Development: Policy Questions* (Washington, DC: National Academy Press).

Vu, M.T. 1985 *World Population Projections 1985: Short- and Long-Term Estimates by Age and Sex with Related Demographic Statistics.* (Baltimore: Johns Hopkins University).

World Bank, 1981. *Accelerated Development in Sub-Saharan Africa: An Agenda for Action,* The World Bank, Washington, DC.

World Bank, 1983a. *Sub-Saharan Africa: Progress Report on Development Prospects and Programs.* The World Bank, Washington, DC.

World Bank, 1983b. *World Tables: The Third Edition, Volume I Economic Data from the Data Files of the World Bank* and *Volume II Social Data from the Data Files of the The World Bank.* (Baltimore: Johns Hopkins University).

World Bank, 1984a. *World Development Report 1984 (New York:* Oxford University).

World Bank, 1984b. *Toward Sustained Development in Sub-Saharan Africa: A Joint Program of Action,* The World Bank, Washington, DC.

World Bank, 1985. *World Development Report 1985* (New York: Oxford University).

World Bank, 1986a. *World Development Report 1986* (New York: Oxford University).
World Bank, 1986b. *Financing Adjustment with Growth in Sub-Saharan Africa, 1986-90*, The World Bank, Washington, DC.
World Bank, 1986c. *The World Bank Annual Report 1986*. The World Bank, Washington, DC.
World Bank, 1986d. *Population Growth and Policies in Sub-Saharan Africa*. The World Bank, Washington, DC.
World Bank, 1986e. *Poverty and Hunger: Issues and Options for Food Security in Developing Countries*, The World Bank, Washington, DC.
World Resources Institute and International Institute for Environment and Development, 1986. *World Resources 1986: An Assessment of the Resource Base that Supports the Global Economy with Data Tables for 146 Countries*. (New York: Basic Books).

Part 3

An Alternative Vision: Four Future Histories

Introduction

For the purpose of better understanding the four future histories that follow, the reader should be reminded that they are all based on the same assumption: that Africa would be able to enjoy more rapid progress in the twenty-first century than the 'conventional wisdom' chapter suggests, hence 'The Big Lift'. Participants arrived at this conclusion after a close examination of the shortcomings inherent in the current perspective and a deliberate effort to identify an alternative, surprising yet credible, end-point for Africa in 2057. The statistical profile of the Big Lift is presented and compared with the figures for 1957 and 1987 and those of the current perspective in table 5. The latter suggest that Africa in 2057 would be about where Greece is today. The Big Lift scenario would put it closer to where Italy is. Though, at first glance, these figures may appear overly optimistic, they are certainly within the realm of possibility, if consideration is given to what has happened in Africa in the twentieth century (which certainly has not been marked only by decline but also by some of the most rapid developments in any part of the world) and to what is currently happening in other Third World regions.

The future histories were written in the course of two days and thus under obvious pressure of time. They are the product of collective thinking by four groups of individuals representing different academic backgrounds and different African countries. In preparing these stories for publications, the editors have not changed them. They essentially stand as they were produced in Kericho. The only changes are editorial, notably to avoid repetition within each story.

The next four chapters should be read *not* with a view to finding the answers to Africa's current difficulties, but to identifying ideas and issues that should be brought on to the research and policy agenda in Africa. Chapter 8 discusses the various 'levers of change' to which these future histories allude. As such, it contains the recommendations by the workshop participants as to what should be considered and further examined in order to enhance the prospect of a better future for Africa in the twenty-first century.

Table 5: Africa in the year 2057: Some indicators of progress

	Actual	Actual	Conventional wisdom	African vision
Demography	**1957**	**1987**	**2057**	**2057**
Total population (million)	270	599	220	2500
Population growth rate (% per year)	2.3	3.1	0.5	1.5
Infant mortality (per 1000)	182	181	10	8
Life expectancy at birth (years)	40	53	77	80
Economy and Agriculture				
GDP per capita (1980 US$)	450	815	3800	7600
Capital goods production (Million 1975 US$)	127	1273	75800	115000
Agricultural production (FAO index)	63	115	1000	2000
Food supply per capita (calories)	2060	2094	3200	6000
Human Resources				
Literacy rate (%)	16	53	80	95
Scientists and technologists (per million inhabitants)	15	103	270	1000
Natural Resources and Environment				
Arable land (million ha)	177	221	365	500
Energy consumption per capita (kg. coal equivalent per person)	180	451	2000	3600
Forested areas (million ha)	1580	1315	920	1500

4
The Big Lift: A Journalist's Account*

It was the eve of the centennial anniversary of Ghana's independence in the year 2057. Kwame, the political analyst of *The New Age*—the predominant English-speaking newspaper in West Africa—had been asked by his chief editor to write a feature article tracing Africa's history since 1957. Going through archival material, Kwame kept asking himself: what would have surprised Nkrumah had he been alive today?

In thinking about what to write Kwame remembered that Nkrumah was really the architect of the euphoric era that characterized the first two decades of political independence. "Seek ye first the political kingdom, and everything else will be added unto ye," Nkrumah's well-known advice to fellow African nationalist leaders was really an invitation to treat political power as the principal mechanism of change. It also became, however, a justification for individual leaders to accumulate wealth through public office and curtail the freedom of others. Although African intellectuals had criticized this phenomenon already in the 1960s, it was allowed to go on for a much longer time because government leaders could take advantage of external funds, whether provided by private or public sources. Although many African government leaders had verbally criticized the conditions under which foreign aid and foreign investment had been extended to Africa in the 1960s and 1970s they were really the prime beneficiaries of these resource transfers. It blinded them to the growing contradictions between state and society, rich and poor, democracy and dictatorship, that emerged in the late 20th century.

The honeymoon period for African governments came to an end in the 1980s and 1990s as private foreign capital moved to other regions of the world and donor funding of government programmes in Africa began to dry up.

For quite some time, African governments continued to plead with the international community, assuming that Africa's future was tied to the provision of external inputs. The weakness of the African economies following the hike in oil prices in the 1970s, the droughts of the 1980s, and the weakening prices of commodities produced in Africa, enabled

*The group composing this version consisted of: Dr. Chinua Achebe, Dr. Goran Hyden, Dr. Calestous Juma, Professor Kwesi Prah and Dr. Mahendra Shah (chair).

the International Monetary Fund—the guardian of the international monetary system of the second part of the 20th century—together with the World Bank to impose measures aimed at restructuring the African economies in the direction of open markets. Because these measures were far too narrowly conceived, they never produced any beneficial changes for Africa. In the late 1980s, African countries began to drop out of the programme and in protest cancel debt service obligations which they found impossible to continue paying. In the end the international community had to accede to this fact, though it sent shock signals through bank circles. The final collapse, however, of what had been known as the Bretton-Woods agreement for global monetary stability occurred in the late 1990s as the combined effects of accumulated debt burdens among Latin American countries and the downfall of the U.S. dollar as the principal global currency, a process that was accelerated in the 1990s by the inability of two subsequent administrations in Washington to reverse the budget deficit and rapidly growing outflow of capital from the U.S.

In reflecting about where Africa was in the late 1980s and early 1990s, Kwame could hardly believe that Africa had made such rapid progress since then. He felt that he could legitimately describe the process in the first part of the 21st century as "the Big Lift." Africa had lifted itself by the bootstraps in a way that nobody had anticipated in the late 20th century. Kwame's Africa of 2.5 billion people was experiencing economic growth per capita at a rate of 8% and its agricultural production had grown twenty times since the crisis of the 1980s. It was now having an industrial base of its own and producing rapidly increasing numbers of scientists and technologists.

Demographically, it was still expanding but at a modest rate of 1.5%, a little lower than other regions of the world. Infant mortality in the past decades, for instance, had shrunk to 14/1000. Though Africa was still on average the poorest continent in the world, it had become an increasingly powerful and respected actor in the international arena. The question that Kwame really wanted to address in his article was: what were the factors that explained Africa's extraordinary progress in the first half of the 21st century?

He realized that it wasn't much of what political leaders and most analysts had stressed in the 20th century. It was rather a combination of the fortuitous circumstances and hard collective will that emerged in the 1990s, as Africa was growing increasingly irrelevant to its traditional partners in the West. With the rapid growth of synthetic production of commodities in the West to replace sugar, cocoa, coffee, etc., Africa's ability to sustain its economies on the basis of export earnings collapsed. In combination with pressure to feed increasing numbers of people, African countries had little choice but to rethink their strategy. This "delinking by default," which was facilitated by the cancellation of the debt service and the new monetary system emerging, created what an increasing number of concerned Africans realized as a unique historical opportunity. It would not have been seized upon, however, had Africa not undergone its own cultural revolution, i.e. a period of extensive self scrutiny.

Growing out of discontent with authoritarian leadership and dismal government performance, Africans in the 1990s shifted from just withdrawing from the formal system of governance towards changing it. Working through non-governmental institutions, educated people across the continent created new movements to start a second liberation of the continent. This effort was largely aided by the abolition of the *apartheid* system in South Africa in 1995 after a severe bloodletting. Although many whites had run away from South Africa and much private capital had fled the country during this period of violence, one of the positive outcomes of this process towards black-majority rule was the speed with which manpower and capital from other countries filled the short-term gaps created by the white exodus. Thus, by the beginning of the 21st Century South Africa (now Azania) had for the first time emerged as a non-racial state. The effect of this change was dramatic in the whole of southern Africa which in the 21st ceentury had developed as the economically most advanced and powerful sub-region on the continent. Southern Africa celebrated the turn of the century by creating SAREC—the Southern Africa Regional Economic Cooperation Agreement—a common market encompassing Azania, Namibia and the members of the now defunct SADCC.

The essence of this new force was the rediscovery of Africa's own culture and what Africans across the continent have in common. As a new pride and self-confidence emerged, and people began to organize themselves for the vital tasks of protecting and developing the continent's resources on a sustainable basis, opposition to arbitrary rule in Africa grew fast. By the 1990s, Africans rejected not only military rule but also the one-party system that had been so dominant in the first three decades of independence. To be sure, as Kwame realized when he read through the archival material, many governments detained and even killed advocates of the "second liberation" movements, yet in the long run, beginning in some of the misgoverned countries, these were able to establish themselves in power and pave the way for greater democracy and delegation of authority to local communities. Africa had by the beginning of the 21st century got its new heroes, a group of political leaders who devised policies that met Africa's needs and respected other people, whether they agreed with them or not. Thinking that this must have been a big surprise for those who followed African politics in the first three decades after independence, Kwame couldn't help quoting a comment by one of Africa's foremost movelists who, in reflecting on the political changes in the late 1990s, had said that for the first time since pre-colonial times political power in Africa was now based on legitimate authority.

But this political reformation was also somewhat unexpectedly facilitated by the growing number of epidemics—notably AIDS and malaria—that affected Africa in the 1990s, partly as a result of the collapse of public health institutions. Before effective vaccines had been developed, Africa had lost large numbers of its people (though not as many as projected in the 1980s). The demographic consequence of this scourge was not only to reduce the population in the 1990s and the early 2000s, but also to spin off a population recovery in the first three decades of the new century. Africa's "baby boom" in those years was largely responsible for the rapid increase that left the continent in the mid-century with 2.5 billion.

The most significant long-term effect of AIDS, however, was not demographic but behavioural. Two related factors contributed to this change. The first was the slow and ineffective way in which African governments responded to the threat of these epidemics. Kwame realized that this insufficient response was partly due to lack of financial resources, but whatever its cause, it left individuals and voluntary organizations to deal with these threats on their own. The second factor was that when governments eventually responded, it was in a panicky, fascist fashion. By this time, however, values had changed in the direction of individual and social discipline, members of society had grown socially conscious of this and other issues, and as a result, people organized themselves against the arbitrary violation of civil rights that several African governments committed in their belated efforts to deal with AIDS. Following on top of many other violations of political rights, the AIDS issue became an unexpected catalyst of democratic change.

It was approximately in 2015 that Africa had completed its difficult period of transition from dictatorship to democracy. This new political era was accompanied by growing creativity and diversity in society, both at the local and governmental levels. Voluntary organizations, cooperatives (not the old state-controlled ones, but the spontaneously created) and African business companies engaged in a wide range of productive investments taking advantage of new locally developed seed varieties, bio-technologies and resource-conserving approaches to growth. One interesting development in the beginning of the 21st century was the growing research capacity in community-based organizations and their role as carriers of more appropriate technology, including agroforestry that began already in the late 20th century. Especially important was the emergence of new co-operative ventures involving crossnational institutions. A few of these had started already in the 20th century but none became significant until the African economies had effectively delinked from the West and began to re-orient themselves to the needs and potentials of the continent. These resource-based ventures among African states were by the mid-21st century the principal sub-regional units of co-operation.

Intra-African trade expanded quite rapidly in the 2020s and 2030s as a result of growth in both agriculture and manufacturing. The expansion of the pan-African highway system which also took place during these years paved the way for greater trade, particularly between East and West Africa. With Nigeria at its core, the latter had emerged as an industrializing region competing with SAREC. The Economic Community of West African States (ECOWAS) never took off in the 20th century and was replaced in the beginning of the 21st century by inter-state cooperation centered on the utilization of riverine resources. Talks of a wider West African market that may stretch as far as East Africa as a means of meeting the competition from SAREC and other industrializing regions of the world had begun in the 2040s. In 2050 the countries in the region formed GROW—the Grouping of River Organizations in West Africa.

It would be difficult, Kwame argued, to explain this phenomenal change in a relatively short period without referring to the driving "myth" that inspired the Africans to make this progress. The lack of collective self-esteem that had characterized the African mind in the 20th century was replaced by a new pride and sense of nationalism that among other things led to the spread and development of African languages following the new avenues of trade and economic co-operation. This process was further aided by advances made in the field of informatics which, among other things, facilitated the development of literature in all major African languages.

It was in this spirit that many other economic activities were redefined in terms of commercial viability and relevance to Africa. For instance, the notion of common currencies that had existed in colonial days was being revived and developed in various parts of the continent. These efforts laid the foundation for the plan for common monetary systems in Africa, one for the members of GROW and another for members of SAREC.

In developing its own industrial base, Africa could take advantage of its rich natural resources. Technological breakthroughs beginning in the 1990s enabled Africa to develop its hydro-electric resources and transmit energy at low rates over long distances. This became an important source of economic progress. Lesotho, for instance, now a key member of SAREC, had become the "powerhouse" of Africa. Perhaps even more remarkable was the increased use of other energy sources, notably solar energy, geo-thermal power, small hydro power stations, bio-gas and other renewable sources. Thus, by the mid-21st century, Africa had a balanced energy mix.

Particularly striking to Kwame was the development of indigenous scientific and technological capacity in Africa in the 21st century. It contrasted sharply with the situation that he read about in the late 20th century when African governments paid little attention to the subject, the IMF told the governments to cut down investments in higher education, and African acientists migrated outside the continent to do their work. Two factors were responsible for the change. One was the growing importance of East and South Asia as sources of new technologies of particular appropriateness to the less industrialized parts of the world. In the 1990s and way into the 21st century large numbers of Africans were trained in other Third World countries, thus acquiring skills that were particularly relevant to the continent's growing agro-based industries. The other factor was that after 2015 when the second liberation was completed, African states began to stress the need for developing indigenous technologies through greater emphasis on local training. Although the process had started earlier in some countries, after 2015 Africa witnessed an indigenous technological revolution. The principal outcomes of these efforts were the development of Africa's resources in such a way that they increasingly met the needs of its peoples and the generation of a growing core of scientific and technological capacity centered both in the productive sectors and in institutions of research.

Against the backdrop of the far-reaching changes associated with the 'Big Lift', it was perhaps surprising that so much of Africa's traditional social organization and structure had survived. Commercialization and industrialization had not wiped out Africa's own cultural and social heritage. The extended family, for instance, and the ethic underpinning it, had been revived in the early 21st century, as part of the "cultural revolution" that Africa experienced at that time. Much like East Asia in the late 20th century, Africa had demonstrated in the second quarter of the 21st century that the road to industrial society does not have to follow the original path of the West. There was now much talk of the "African way" of development, implying a form of capitalism (that term is still with us) with a "human face." Particularly significant in the African approach was the ability of society to organize its social welfare activities on a private, yet cooperative and egalitarian basis, thus avoiding the bureaucratization of care that was the hallmark of Europe's mode of development in the 20th century.

African women had for a long time fought an uphill struggle for greater social and political recognition. The second liberation in the early 21st century that cut across all sectors of society finally permitted a major breakthrough for the women. Organized and militant in outlook, African women's organizations managed in the 2020s to secure favourable quotas for admission of young women into institutions of higher learning, especially in the fields of science and engineering. As a report issued on the 50th anniversary of the Nairobi Women's Conference in 2035 stated: "Compared to any other region of the world, African women have made the most remarkable progress since the gender issue was globalized in the 1970s."

Kwame wanted to place particular emphasis on the great strides forward that Africa had made since the turn of the century but he was also aware of the costs that had been incurred and the threats inherent in the global system. As a result of the transformation that had taken place, there had been wars, political upheavals and loss of human life. It was wrong, he kept telling himself, to assume that Africa had "arrived", that it had solved all its problems. Africa was still struggling with a harsh environment but the difference was that the continent's own people were now able to cope with these challenges on the basis of their own strength. Furthermore, Africa had to pay dearly for the costs of its progress, but when reflecting on it, Kwame realized that these costs were probably more acceptable than the costs Africa paid as a neo-colonial underdog before the second liberation was completed. He read that in the beginning of the 21st century Africans generally accepted that foreign aid had largely been a trap that had held back the continent's progress by forcing upon its people solutions that were irrelevant. To be sure, a few donors had in the 1990s accepted the shortcomings of such foreign aid and had begun to provide aid that was supportive of the growth of African initiatives, whether in the cultural or material sphere.

One serious threat to Africa in the 2030s and 2040s had been the aggressive behaviour of other industrializing regions of the world. South Korea and Brazil had since long joined the group of industrialized countries but other countries in both Latin America and Asia were engaged in fierce competition with Africa. Through the presence of larger internal markets Africa could absorb some of these threats without being thrown off balance but the competition among the industrializing countries constituted even in the 2050s a major element of uncertainty.

The biggest threat of all, however, Africa shared with the rest of humankind: biological warfare. It had replaced nuclear weapons as the principal instrument of war. It was particularly difficult to control as it was available not only to governments but also to private individuals. A particularly ugly incident took place in a Central African country in 2019 when an experiment conducted by a group of scientists went out of control and caused the death of two million people over the next few years. By 2035 the pressure to find means of controlling the use of biology for destructive purposes had grown to such an extent that a special international police agency had been set up to monitor and control activities conducted by governments and individuals. Still, the possibility of detecting the smoke of the biological gun was often elusive and for Africans as well as others this threat constituted the main fear under which they lived in the year 2057.

5

The Big Lift: A Scientist's Reflections*

Introduction

Distinguished ladies and gentlemen, I wish to thank the Rector of Makerere University here in the Federation of East Africa for his kind invitation to address you on this august occasion, another landmark in the overall development of science and techonology on this continent. To Africa's great scientists, engineers and techonologists, who have contributed in making this day a reality, I also extend my warm appreciation and congratulations for building what we are convinved will undoubtely become one of the world's most advanced institutes for aeronautics and space science research.

I have chosen the topic of my address 'Africa in the past seventy years' for obvious reasons. As we move forward technologically and otherwise with the rest of the world, it is often useful to review the past in order to take full advantage of what we are at the moment and avoid repeating the mistakes of the past.

It is refreshing to state that Africa today (June 3, 2057) is an economically expanding region of the world with a population of 2.5 billion, an average growth rate of 8 per cent per annum and an average per capita income of US$7,600. There are, as you know, mountains of corn, millet, rice, etc., everywhere and not a child in the continent is suffering from malnutrition! Beautiful healthy babies can be seen in even the remotest villages. Our infant mortality is at its lowest ebb. It is well known that the infant mortality rate on this continent is one of the lowest in the whole world!

African high technology industries designed and maintained by our scientists, technologists, and our skilled labour, produce to meet our basic needs in the fields of agriculture, health, housing, etc. In quantitative terms, the ratio of our scientists to technicians has now reached 1 to 15. In other words, we have about 1,200 scientists and 18,000 technicians per million inhabitants respectively.

*The Group composing this version consisted of: Professor Deborah E. Akaiye, Professor Biniakamu Dia Dianzungu, Dr Kabiru Kinyanjui (Chair), Dr Thandika Mkandawire and Dr Cyrus Mutiso.

Politically, we have democratic regional governments which respect the dignity of our peoples, and fundamental human rights are entrenched in our constitutions as well as actively practised. When there have been cases of the violation of human rights, they have been investigated and victims of such violations have found redress in our system of justice.

Looking back on the last seventy years, we can see that Africa has arrived at this enviable position not without tears, blood and struggle. This is indeed a story of the triumph of the human spirit!

There have been basically four identifiable periods in this long struggle. First were the years between 1987 and 1995 which our children now refer to as the 'International Monetary Fund (IMF) years' or 'years of blood, sweat and tears', during which African nations were at the mercy of the manipulations of the IMF and the World Bank.

Then came the period between 1995 and 2015 when African nations rejected loans from the IMF and the World Bank, were consequently abandoned, as it were, by the industrial north to their own destiny and forced to look inwards for their material and other needs. Out of this, the spirit of African self-reliance and creativity in all spheres of human endeavour emerged.

The next period 2015-20 were the years of consolidation bringing into being genuine regional co-operation among African states. This enhanced our industrial and agricultural "revolution" thereby ushering in a period of tremendous social, economic and technological development.

The fourth period, 2020-57, is the period which most of you are familiar with. Africa's accomplishments in the last few decades in the fields of science, industry, culture, agriculture and health and in her contributions to world peace are well known. Our contributions to social justice both within and outside the continent are without parallel in the history of mankind. The emancipation of African women has served as a catalyst, bringing new energies, talents and visions to all aspects of our developments.

Let us now take a closer look at the various dimensions of our development in the last seventy years, that is, from 1987 to 2057. These will be considered under the sub-headings "Economic trends", "State and political process", "Science and technology", "Gender," "Religion," "Language", and "Cultural trends".

Economic Trends

In reviewing the economic trends in Africa during the period 1987-95 it is pertinent to note that during the first ten to twelve years after independence, that is from 1957-70, African economies enjoyed high rates of growth. Rates of industrialization (7-7.2 per cent) were as high as in other developing countries. Export crop production continued to increase although signs of crisis in food production were visible. The world recession which started in the mid-seventies led to a lot of serious economic problems for Africa. By 1980-85, African countries became increasingly dependent on foreign finance.

Following investments in the social sector in the post-independence period there was significant improvement in life expectancy, and infant mortality declined. A number of African countries saw their population growth rate rise to as high as 4.1 per cent. In response to the growth of industry and service in the urban areas, there was an acceleration in the rate of urbanization.

By 1990, virtually all African countries had entered into some kind of structural adjustment programmes (SAP) which involved devaluation of currencies, reducing of social expenditure, removal of protection for industries, etc. As had been feared by most African governments, these measures were recessionary as a result of decline in investment and in most cases, net outflow of capital. For the entire period, per capita income declined by 1 per cent to US$ 752 by 1995.

One effect of the SAP was an improvement of terms of trade for agriculture as a whole. Commercial agriculture increased its production substantially. Peasant agriculture also responded positively although it was severely limited by low technology. As a consequence of improved returns in food production, men re-entered food production in great numbers. Significantly, a number of retiring bureaucrats found agriculture very lucrative and began to invest in food production specially for the domestic market. Low world prices for export crops led to a general shift towards production for the domestic market.

As a result of the removal of protection, the collapse of urban incomes and movements of terms of trade against industry, there was a massive breakdown and under-utilization of industrial capacity. This led to a process of "de-industrialization" and serious urban crisis — crime, unemployment, etc. As a result there was increased "informalization" of production and services.

Population growth was 2.7 per cent and infant mortality increased sharply as a result of poor social services.

Between 1995 and 2015 the economy stagnated and had zero growth. The decline of industry continued although agricultural production was steady, barely keeping up with population growth. Infant mortality continued to increase as a result of further decline in social services.

Demographically, the process of urbanization was reversed and replaced by the "ruralization" of urban areas, as urban and peri-urban small-scale farming increased.

The informalization of economic activities continued and assumed a more innovative and structured form in particular as they were controlled by various mutual support groups and associations.

Between 2015-20 the growth rate picked up substantially reaching up to 5 per cent. The improvement was triggered by increased agricultural production and agro-based industrialization based on locally derived science and technology.

Improved growth rate facilitated the financing of social services which led to reduced infant mortality and increased population growth.

Finally during the last thirty-seven years, that is between 2020 and 57, the economy enjoyed an 8 per cent per annum growth rate, leading to a 200 per cent growth of the economy every nine years. Agriculture enjoyed a high growth rate based on the increased use of locally produced industrial inputs.

Infant mortality rates have fallen to rates prevalent in all other parts of the world.

State and Political Process

1987-95 was the period during which African states groaned under the yoke of IMF/World Bank loans with their austerity measures resulting in falling wages, unemployment, increasing crime, food riots, falling educational and health standards, etc. Because of the unpopularity of these austerity measures and increasing conflict between capital and labour, and amongst capital, the state and peasantry over land matters arising from increased penetration and acquisition of land by retiring bureaucrats and trans-national agrobusiness, African states became increasingly authoritarian.

There was also an unprecedented militarization of social life, leading to the dehumanization of all aspects of society and the blatant violation of fundamental human rights. The states sought to atomise society by undue control and surveillance. Civil society was thus increasingly compelled to resort to its own collective means of material and spiritual survival. There was a lot of pressure on African governments to accept schemes that were environmentally degrading such as nuclear power plants, storage and waste disposal and also "dirty" bio-technological and genetic engineering industries. These attempts were resisted by African states because of the consciousness of a few African patriots.

Regional and co-operation schemes and initiatives were shelved by individual states as structural adjustment strategies took hold. Consequently African states retreated from Pan-Africanism.

Between 1995 and 2015 the failure of export-oriented strategies and the lack of the political legitimacy of African governments led to popular democratic struggles. There was a collapse of authoritarian and military regimes and popular rejection of IMF programmes. These led to the creation of populist and nationalist regimes.

During this period, foreign capital was no longer interested in African states which were unable to pay their debts. Africa was thus more "marginalized" in the international system. Consequently, African governments reintroduced the question of regional co-operation as a process of dealing with the economic crisis. Elements of democratization started to emerge in all African states.

Social movements (religious, mutual support groups, co-operatives, and other non-governmental organizations) which emerged to fill the space left by the collapse of state structures were active in the process of democratization of the states. No single movement was dominant during this period. There was tremendous social experimentation in participation and democratization at grassroot levels which transcended national boundaries. These initiatives were to become the seeds of the true Pan-Africanism as we know it today.

The period 2015-20 was characterized by the emergence of popular forms of Pan-Africanism. The logic of economic recovery compelled the ruling elites to accept regional co-operation and democratization of the state as the norm.

The state emerged as the moderator of civil groups in society and the guardian of democratic gains acquired in the previous period. Specifically, the state in this period was not the dominant actor in society. Hence the state was "tamed" by civil society.

During the period 2020-57, African states have become democratic, international, and Pan-African. There are the Pan-African Common Market, Common Market Council, African Human Rights Council, African Court of Justice, African Council for Advanced Science and Technology, which are now all well established.

In the international sphere, African governments are no longer subservient to foreign interests and thereby interact with the rest of the world on the basis of mutual benefit and respect.

Science and Technology

The development of science and technology in Africa during the past seventy years is even more interesting. In the period 1987-95, African governments desperate for development under the yoke of the IMF encouraged all sorts of "quacks" to carry out experiments in what was called "appropriate technology" in numerous villages and urban centres in Africa.

Universities all over Africa systematically declined in the critical areas of science and technology. Science-based departments in the universities and polytechnics became so poorly equipped that no meaningful teaching and research programmes were undertaken. Scientific literacy even at the primary and secondary levels declined considerably, to the extent that no science subjects were taught. The best trained African scientists and engineers migrated to the north for better employment opportunities, thereby undermining African scientific and technological capabilities.

Simultaneously, informal sectors began to adapt, repair, and maintain equipment and machines and in addition, to improvise and introduce innovations as needed. These processes of improvisation and innovation generated new indigenous "scientific and technological languages" and know-how.

1995-2015 was clearly the period of the demystification and democratization of élite-oriented science and technology and also of formal higher education. Imported equipment was cannibalized to repair and make new machines. There was in evidence a slow but steady increase in local expertise and innovations replacing "formal" technical assitance programmes.

Several formally trained engineers and scientists were forced to join the informal sectors and were recycled, thus reducing the gap between the formally trained scientists and technologists on the one hand and the indigeous technocrats on the other.

The "been-tos" returned to Africa in very large numbers and the "brain-drain" became a thing of the past as locally trained scientists and engineers were considered "poorly trained" by foreign markets. African science and technology thus became culturalized, accepted and respected locally as a result of necessity and the need for self-reliance.

Between 2015-20 the experiences of the previous period became integrated into the educational system.

During the period 2020-57 large-scale industrialization developed in the previous period became a major force for regional co-operation. By this time, Africa had realized its enormous energy potential and had therefore directed its science and technology towards the harnessing and effective utilization of this energy for high technology industrialization. Africa's appreciation of the role of high technology in its overall development led to the creation of Pan-African centres of excellence in training research and development in this field.

African universities and polytechnics have emerged, based on culturally sound science and technology. These institutions are well-equipped and are now centres of excellence in their own right.

Gender

The role of African women in the overall development of Africa has been a topical issue during the seventy year period under review. During the period 1987-95, the problem of marginalization and degradation of women became pronounced as a result of the negative effects of structural adjustment programmes. The family hardships that ensued were manifested in such vices as prostitution, child labour, family stress and single parenthood. This was in spite of the then popular rhetoric for the emancipation of women. As is always the case in a situation of stress, the more oppressed groups bear most of the burden.

Thus, although there was a feminist movement and other popular resistance to this degradation, there were only a few symbolic acts such as the appointment of a female minister in the twenty-four male cabinet of one nation, and of a female permanent secretary to the head of state in another country. Those few palliative measures made very little impact on the general, oppressive trend.

Changes in the agrarian industry towards export-oriented crops resulted in rural women becoming sources of cheap labour in commercialized agriculture.

The situation of women in education during this period also worsened. Because of exorbitant school fees and the privatization of schools, girls were withdrawn from schools and in general the positions of women as teachers and/or pupils were adversely affected.

Between 1995 and 2015 there came the collapse of tourism and growing resentment to the degradation of women by means of popular movements. Two conflicting responses emerged: first, a strong egalitarian tendency in favour of women's emancipation as in most millenial movements, and secondly, authoritarian and paternalistic practices patronizing women. These conflicts persisted in and characterized African society.

Between 2015 and 2020 due to emerging favourable trends in education and in economic and agricultural development which were reflected in culture and religion, the paternalistic and male chauvinistic tendencies were seriously undermined. This was part and parcel of the democratization of the society. Questions of gender and equality were now central issues of debate. They however were not resolved to the satisfaction of the majority of women.

In the last thirty or so years, 2020-57, it can be shown through the usual social indicators such as employment opportunities, access to education, control and ownership of agricultural and industrial production, and access to leadership positions, that the position of women in African society has improved. Yet there is still room for improvement.

Religion

Religion has always played an important role in the social lives of our people. During the period 1987-95 African societies spent less on social services and subsidized goods. This, coupled with the "opening up" of the economy to foreign investment, led to what Africans used to call "collective colonialism".

The ensuing economic crisis provoked a whole range of cultural responses. Fundamentalist movements grew and ethnic conflicts were exacerbated. Because of stress, escapist millenial movements and indigenous African religious groups emerged. Also notable during this period was an increase in supernatural explanations of the African situation. Fundamentalist religious groups were manipulated by outsiders — both Moslem and Christian. Religious fervour during this period also assumed ethnic identification, thereby creating greater stress and ethnic-religious conflicts.

The emergence of 'Kimbanguist' movements seeking to marry science, culture and religious expression were positive outcomes during those difficult years. These developments tended to exclude the orthodox organized religions, although for their survival they were compelled to Africanize their rituals and forms of worship, and to make their messages relevant to the socio-economic aspirations of ordinary people.

These movements, because of their popular base and simple lifestyles, created problems for the authoritarian and military states. These organizations, by their nature, were more participatory in and receptive to the needs of the popular masses in terms of health, education, housing etc. Because of their austere life-style and collective commitment to the community's well-being, they were able to generate high levels of savings which were utilized in community services.

Between 1995-2015, the grassroot movements of the previous period became the "signs of hope" during these years, and were taken very seriously by the people. Thus they became dominant in the local communities. Politically, they became respectable and in some states they were viewed as the authentic voice of the ordinary people. They started agitating for representation at all levels of decision-making in the society. In this way, they formed the base on which respect and tolerance for diversity of religion was built. This tolerance was consequently practised in many African states. Africa during this period looked inwards to drink from the wells and springs of its own culture and religion.

In the period 2015-20 African states became reconciled to their religious diversity and more respect for individual religious affiliation was observable. Secularization of institutions which remained from previous periods was emphasized during this era. A significant proportion of the total production in the society came from these groups and from economic institutions which had their base at the community level. These groups also started to provide leaders to other societal institutions. Increased religious tolerance was noted. The seeds of Pan-African religious linkages from grassroot groups were sown during this period.

In the last thirty years or so, 2020-57, African-based religions have increasingly been transmitted to different parts of the world and thereby have found linkages with similar religious movements of the African diaspora. There have thus emerged various versions of African religions which are less apologetic about themselves. As you very well known, many Europeans are now coming to learn and be inspired by this African heritage. They are being assimilated in the process.

Language

Languages are powerful tools of communication. During the period 1987-95, English, French, Portuguese and Arabic remained the dominant languages of politics, economics, commerce, science and education.

Due to IMF/World Bank educational policies which were forced on African societies, there was, as earlier mentioned, a collapse of the educational system, leading to the poor teaching of these "classical or élitist" languages in town and village educational institutions. Lack of textbooks was evident in all schools and these languages tended to be pidginized in the way they were taught or spoken. On the other hand, there emerged cheap novels and pamphlets in local languages.

At the state level, officials were forced to continue to use the elitist languages in order to be able to communicate with the rest of the world. Thus, these languages were spoken and written in a "better" form by only a minority of the élite.

Local religious movements used local languages and produced more reading materials and they therefore became agents of the propagation of education and technology in local languages.

Intellectual movements involving writing in local African languages also gained momentum during this period and by 1995 they had become a major force in the development of African languages.

The mass media abandoned the use of foreign languages towards the end of the period. This trend coupled with the pressure which religious movements exerted led to the increased use of and development of African languages which the mass media incorporated and popularized.

Between 1995 and 2015 there was a general intensification of the processes initiated in the previous period. A movement for the translation of scientific works and foreign literature into local languages gained momentum during the period. Publishing houses which specialized in African languages experienced a boom industry. Fascination with learing African languages was fostered in schools, mosques and villages.

During the period 2015-20, African languages were introduced in the learning processes at all levels of education and training.

Finally, in the years 2020-57 due to an increase in trans-national co-operation etc., a few African languages such as Hausa, Swahili and Lingala began to be more widely spoken. Because of the economic prosperity of this period, language policy was given much attention in the various regions of Africa. English, French and Portuguese, as you know, are now languages confined to universities and spoken only by a small minority of the African elite whose work requires them to communicate in those languages.

Major centres for learning of Hausa, Swahili, Lingala, a new Bantu-based lingua franca of Southern Africa and other African languages have emerged and are thriving very well. These are now the dominant languages for education, commerce, trade, and politics in the continent. These languages are also internationally recognized.

Cultural Trends

Culture as a dynamic and living phenomenon witnessed tremendous changes in Africa during the whole period of the seventy years under review.

In considering the period 1985-95, it is worth noting that during the the IMF era "culture" continued to be a tourist and élite pastime activity from which the masses of the people were excluded. However, a counter culture later emerged, expressing itself in dances, ceremonies, burials, wedding, etc. It found unique expression and form in urban and rural areas. These cultural expressions were authentic African creations in the changing circumstances of that time. The "tourist culture" led to prostitution and the formalization and commercialization of African culture for the entertainment of foreign tourists and their mimic bourgeois class.

Cultural expression in music, dance and theatre led to the marginalization of élite cultural institutions and books written in foreign languages. The opportunities effected by the informatic revolution induced the rapid growth and expansion of the cultural phenomena which eventually became dominant on the continent.

During the period 1995-2015, the counter-culture became dominant, was expressed in various languages of the African peoples, and was supported and linked to the formal structures of education, religion, theatre and the media. These cultural outcomes were later related and linked to production processes at all levels.

Similarly, between 2015 and 2020 the same processes and developments as in the previous period were continued and entrenched.

Since the period 2020-57, African culture has become one of the dominant world cultures with dynamic expression in music, dance, theatre, film, literature and other cultural forms.

Senghor's dream of African culture becoming a world culture is finally fulfilled!

Conclusion

In conclusion, the major social and economic changes in the last seventy years in Africa are now well known. Our average growth rate of 8 per cent per annum and an average per capita income of US$ 7,600 etc. compare very favourably with those in other parts of the world. This Institute of Advanced Aeronautics and Space Science and Technology is a typical example of the achievements of our scientists and engineers. The wheel of progress is certainly in full motion. Let us all make our contribution to keeping the wheel moving in the right direction!

6

The Big Lift: Kericho Revisited*

Introduction

Over the last seventy years, the Kericho conference has served as a continuing source of thought, inspiration, science and scholarship in the service of a better future for Africa. Meeting every two or three years, with the exception of several difficult years in the time of troubles, the conference addresses topics critical to the future of Africa.

For the twenty-fifth conference, on the seventieth anniversary of the original Kericho conference, the topic is a retrospective examination of the current situation in Africa in the light of the predictions made by the original group of nineteen scholars who met in Kericho in 1987. Their report, entitled "Beyond Hunger: An African Vision", presented the first African image at that time of what the future could be.

The year is 2057. We are at Kericho Tea Hotel in Kenya. We have come together to review the current situation in the light of the predictions made by the group of scholars who met at this hotel in 1987 to ponder a better future for Africa and present images of what that future could be.

Africa in the year 2057 is an economically expanding region of the world. Its total continental population stands at 2.5 billion, five times its population size in 1987, and earns an average per capita income of $7,600 (PTA currency), twice the level projected by the "conventional wisdom" in 1987. Agriculture has grown twenty times since the 1980s and there is a vigorous growth of industry, which has increased by a factor of eighty (80) since 1987. The number of indigenous scientists has risen to 6 million, six times the number recorded in 1987 and there

---

*The group composing this version consisted of: Dr Achola Pala Okeyo, Professor Robert Kates, Professor S. Ojo and Dr Nomtheto Simelane (Chair).

is a newly growing cadre of technical experts numbering 9 million. Infant mortality has dropped remarkably and is as low as anywhere in the world.

1957-90

The sets of circumstances described above came about in the form of a series of distinct periods marked first by the extreme euphoria and idealism of the 1950s to 1970s which characterized the period immediately before and after independence. Political independence was achieved by the majority of African countries (starting with the Sudan in 1956 and with Ghana in 1957 led by the charismatic Kwame Nkrumah). This period of euphoria was later followed by a sharp decline in optimism caused by a more realistic assessment of the real problems (political and social) which faced the continent. This was the period of troubles whose distinctive feature was the erosion of confidence among the mass of the African people consequent upon the recognition that the State apparatus as constituted was really not able to achieve its named objectives.

This failure to achieve stated goals arose from a number of related problems. First and foremost, difficulties arose among the ruling élite in the sharing of power, which led to a questioning of the legitimacy of the leaders by the military and the bureaucratic élites. These contentions led to a failure to institutionalize the democratic process and to the over-bureaucratization of government as it increasingly served as a source of employment. Because the State was seen as the resource manager for development, it led to a quick shift away from the multi-party concept which was perceived initially as a major characteristic of a democratic society.

The State was moreover imposed on the people in such a way as to negate basic cultural affinities and thus wedge itself between peoples who shared a common heritage. This development led to a perverse kind of nationalism which manifested itself in ethnic solidarity at the expense of the broader based principle of social organization and which fell prey to actors in the power game.

In the meantime, the nascent State apparatus was not able to deliver economic solutions to pressing economic problems. Dependency on single crops intensified as did export orientation at the expense of local food self-sufficiency and the development of a domestic market. The overemphasis on foreign exchange earning led to an unprecedented rise in food imports as a result of shortage in grains and cereals. Inimical exogenous factors such as drought, international tariffs, poor terms of trade and recession combined with declining productivity and led to a crisis in the 1980s. The oil crisis of the early seventies threw African economies off-balance with prices of both consumer and capital goods escalating and foreign exchange earning declining as a result of decreasing exports. Industrial development came to a halt as spare parts for machinery could no longer be afforded in the prevailing economic circumstances. Consumer goods became scarce and living standards fell drastically. Africa literally entered a gloomy and dismal period, initially held to a ransom by international agencies such as the IMF and the World Bank. Social policies became the playground of these two financing organizations and political and social crises became the order of the day as a result of their interference.

There collapsed in the 1980s the basic premises of African development made by African leaders in the post-independence era such as the emphasis on formal education (which had led to the increased burden of education expenditure on the national budget), the adherence to the "trickle down" theory of development, and the neglect of internal forces of change. The agricultural labour force began declining parallel with sharp increases in urban sector jobs, sapping agriculture of needed workers and creating pressure on female labour. This was the beginning of the feminization of the agricultural sector.

The social processes arising from the development assumptions and policies of this era resulted in the intensive mobilization of people, especially women and the young, to support the political leadership in exchange for welfarist programmes. Problems associated with undifferentiated education began to emerge as the policy of equality of opportunity became eroded, principally because job opportunities and educational institutions did not correspond to the mobilization zeal manifested at the political level.

Thus, while agriculture had its growth slowed by a negative price structure in favour of the urban sector, no technological breakthroughs were experienced in the crops that were of greatest importance as food staples in the region, namely millet, sorghum and maize. Moreover, the results of the green revolution in wheat and rice in Asia were not easily transferable to Africa because the packages were not adapted to African ecology with its water problems and poor soils requiring greater use of fertilizer.

These factors led to greater lack of confidence that the leadership would deliver the goods and to the governments' increasing preoccupation with security and not the main goals of development set out in the beginning. In the meantime, demographic pressure increased due to improved health care and expanded targeted disease control and immunization programmes supported by the United Nations (WHO) and private interests sympathetic to the region.

At the level of culture and people's psycho-social conditions, the series of changes triggered off by power struggles and perverted ethnic questions led to diminished self-esteem and the destroyed hopes of many. Universities lost in esteem because of the growing suspicion by the contenders for power that the university students and lecturers were troublemakers. In this period, too, inflationary trends eroded working people's income and thus the issue of survival became more critical.

Traditional forms of social organization were thus usurped and used to reinforce a leadership that had clearly failed to achieve its development goals beyond its messianic orientation: the state of the empty shell without the egg had been reached. Traditional symbols were being used to maintain power and this further perverted the role of culture as a basic force in the development of a new Africa.

1990-2020

In 1990-2020 the stark experiences of the period between 1950 and 1980 are re-examined and lessons drawn from them. This is a period of contemplation and reworking the issues to see how we went wrong and how we could move forward. Under the auspices of the African Academy of Sciences, the biennial Kericho conference is transformed into an ongoing activity by the creation of the Pan-African Institute of Advanced Studies, now the host of these important conferences.

At the same time, a series of continuing catastrophes leads to complete desperation. What is known in scientific circles as "the thirty years drought", the longest sequence of dry years in the last four centuries, 1968-1998, seriously limits Africa's ability to move ahead. Despite intermittent years of bumper crops and self-sufficiency, a harbinger of future possibilities, the reliance on grain imports rises disastrously. Self-sufficiency in agriculture declines from 96 per in 1957 to 53 per cent in 1998. The Pala blight of 1992 attacks major export tree crops in six countries, locally devastating the agricultural export economy.

The struggle in South Africa intensifies bringing increasing support and solidarity from the frontline states. This development in turn influences the South African regime to resort to more desperate and extreme measures, the outcome of which is the bombing of four capitals in the frontline states.

The drastic action taken by South Africa angers the African people even more. Solidarity from Africa converts into serious mobilization of material and other support by the frontline states whose call to the international community becomes even more insistent and urgent. The outcome of all these efforts is that the Western world, particularly Britain, which had been an unwilling horse, agrees to impose comprehensive sanctions against South Africa. The internal democratic movement gains momentum and a combination of all these pressures eventually brings South Africa to its knees and South Africa joins the free nations in Africa as a free and democratic state whose immense material resources become available to the rest of Africa.

This Africa of 2057 is one in which the African self-image is greatly enhanced. Africans are proud to be who they are; and there are no donors, just friendly nations and equal partners in international trade. Women are well-represented in major decision-making positions, yet they retain their unique confidence and pleasant gentleness. They are able to enter commerce and public life at a much earlier age because of having fewer children. There is a woman head of state in one country, Tanzania. The clash between religious fundamentalism and feminist issues has led to the greater liberation of women from Islamic principles. A chain of supermarkets called Mami Yoko, established within the framework of the PTA, is owned by a group of market women.

There are a number of scientific discoveries in geophysics and agricultural sciences enabling the region to engage in more advanced food processing and storage. There is a food surplus which is now freely moved around through the regional markets. There is also a breakthrough in parapsychology enabling the parascientific prediction of the future and reshaping of events, and the improvement in health care in areas such as mental health. Stress relief of stress-related diseases through manipulation of systematic investigations into African symbolic culture have led to newer and cheaper ways of water deriving, treatment and management of stress-related and genetic psyclimatic diseases. There are village centres where urban peoples study these practices under well-defined methodologies which have now become widely accepted.

There is a spirit of reconstruction and rejuvenation: *Mluzi* (Ibo); *Kulungisa* (Swazi); *Loso* (Dholuo); *Kugazinza* (Shona). Africa has developed a strong science policy within the framework of the African Academy of Sciences which has integrated parapsychology, science and technology. This has led to other discoveries in the field of agriculture, medicine and health care. We eat healthier food and use natural methods of food growing and non-chemical methods of pest control. Managerial skills at the village level have increased and farmers are able to seek out and use scientific advances to improve agriculture. Agricultural extension has been rendered obsolete. The villagers are conducting learn-to-do-it-yourself programmes in agriculture, health and industry. Togo has emerged as the business centre on the west coast, Kenya in the east and Botswana in the south. Transport within Africa is easy and accessible.

Africa is patenting its own discoveries and producing them in copyright publications under authors and institutions domiciled in Africa. There is a strong language policy which enables research and technology to be incorporated in village level practices. A Pan-African language research and study centre has been established in Arusha *(the Shabaan Robert Research and Study Centre of Languages and Culture).* This happened in the year 2012. Research and scientific technology are being used as a means of transmitting Pan-African languages, including Kiswahili, Hausa, Arabic, together with Portuguese, Chinese and Japanese.

Tanzania is exporting language kits out of the Shabaan Robert Language Research and Study Centre. Children are free to learn Hausa, Arabic, Swahili, English, French, Portuguese, Chinese and Japanese. These languages are being offered in language schools: multilingualism has arrived. The era of religious freedom and a greater human rights consciousness is here. Our scientific research priorities coincide with the needs of the region and we are able to make analyses of GDP which include all aspects of production in the villages.

We have a large number of books written for children in the local languages and translated into several other African languages. Prostitution has disappeared and the tourist trade has changed and dignifies Africa. The film industry has many good images of Africa and negative images have been all erased from the arts. There is a regular African festival of arts and of scientific innovations.

In 1997 Africa experienced a new oil crisis as a result of the depletion of the oil resources of Nigeria and the North Sea and certain Persian Gulf sources. The oil crisis resulted in considerable hardships to African economies. Transportation costs escalated by 30 per cent over 1987 prices and overall costs of living increased by more than 40 per cent.

The harsh economic conditions triggered urban riots and intense political instability throughout Africa, leading to greater political repression and gloom about the future.

By the year 2010, however, things begin to change. The thirty years drought reverses itself dramatically. The increase in carbon-dioxide accumulated in the atmosphere, which began with the use of coal during the industrial revolution, has led to a doubling in carbon-dioxide since the pre-industrial period. Combined with other trace gases, this greenhouse effect has led to a global warming, which was unambiguously observed by the year 1994.

Within this warming trend there is great climatic diversity, the warmer conditions leading to new agricultural possibilities in the northern lands of Canada, the USSR and Scandinavia; to drying in the middle temperature grain belts in the US, USSR and China; and to more moisture in Africa on both sides of the Sahara and along the arid and semi-arid lands of eastern and southern Africa. Vegetation appears in the Sahara and the Kalahari region reaching the so-called climatic optimum of 6-4,000 years B.C. The first wheat exports to China from Zambia move through Luthuli Bay (formerly known as Richard Bay), the major Azanian grain port.

The energy situation is drastically transformed by the discovery of the Rift fields of oil and gas along the Great Rift Valley, beginning with the Lake Tanganyika find of 1993. Simultaneously, the great superconductive discoveries of 1987-91 make feasible the long range transmission of hydroelectric power. New dams planned in the early 1990s for the Congo, Niger and Zambesi basins begin to come on line in 2005-15.

Cheap electricity supplying a denser population network fuels a major development of new heavy industry. The new Chivizi electric steel process, smelting at low atmospheres, makes possible the development of three heavy industry constellations centred in Benoni, Azania, in Mbeya, Tanzania, and in Boma, Zaire.

As heavy industry grows, high technological development takes three different and somewhat surprising forms: (1) information techniques specializing in speech, translation, and the portable speech video transmission; (2) the joint Euro-African aerospace effort utilizing the ample testing and construction sites of the Northern Sahel; and (3) biotechnology based on banana fermentation.

We have spent more time on the years before 2020 mainly because those were the critical ones for Africa. It was in that period, particularly in the early years of this century, that the foundation of our current growth and success was laid. Thus, we make no apology for having concentrated our presentation on the earlier rather than the latter part of the centennial period we are reflecting on today.

7

The Big Lift: A Report to the Organization of African Unity*

Address to the OAU by the Secretary General, on the centenary of the Independence of Ghana.
(NOTE: the report was due in 2056, but the OAU Secretariat requested that it be presented on 6 March 2057, to mark the 100 years of Ghana's independence.)

Introduction

On this memorable day, March 6, year 2057, we celebrate the first of a series of events that led to the liberation of Africa from colonial rule by European states, a colonial rule that started as early as the fifteenth century and in some countries lasted for over three hundred years, to be vanquished after much bloodshed. Honourable ministers, today we celebrate the centenary of the independence of Ghana from British rule. It was on the sixth of March 1957 that Kwame Nkrumah emerged from the prison of the Gold Coast to become the first prime minister of Ghana. Kwame had fired the first signal shot of the war of the sovereignty of African nations, a war whose battles raged for well nigh half a century till the liberation of Azania.

But Kwame was to die a disappointed man, a man exiled from the land he had so dearly loved. Ghana reached a political turmoil with its economy completely shattered. Nkrumah was not only heartbroken by the events in Ghana: he had seen sister countries like Nigeria, that had held so much hope, derailed from the golden path of free Africa; Zaire

---

*The group composing this version consisted of: Dr Hussein Adam (chairman), Dr Michael Chege, Ms Rosemary Jommo and Dr Christopher Magadza.

was stillborn. His vision, the United States of Africa, seemed irredeemably erased. Well before his physical death Nkrumah had died a spiritual death.

Honourable ministers, let us reflect a little. Let us imagine Africa revisited. Let us see standing before us in this august gathering here today that founding father, Kwame Nkrumah. What Africa would we present to him? What would he frown at? Smile at? Jest about?

You no doubt recall the number of studies on the African future that were undertaken in the 1980s. The United Nations world population prospects projected 1.6 billion inhabitants on the African continent by the year 2025. The World Watch Institute in 1984 portrayed an Africa on a fast train to starvation. The FAO Atlas on African Agriculture showed large parts of Africa with a negative GNP, declining food security, high infant mortality and a life expectancy of 66 years for the well-to-do countries and as low as 34 years for the not so fortunate. At the special United Nations General Assembly of 1986, which was called to discuss the African crisis, its leaders were blatantly displayed as inept begging demagogues who were in no position to lay down any conditions to the then developed countries. The United Nations Environment Programme studies on desertification in the late 1970s showed a withering Africa with no prospect of respite... an Africa groaning "Oh my people, what have I done to you?".

Today, March 6, 2057, I, Nonkululeko Mandela, grand-daughter of Kwame's contemporary, Nelson Mandela, who unlike Kwame died in the darkness of the last of the symbols of colonialism, the Robben Island jail, am proud to present to Kwame... "Nkrumah rediscovered" I am proud to present him an Africa with a vibrant economy, an Africa with a rich cultural heritage, an Africa with food security, an Africa united in purpose, an Africa respected among other human races.

Africa today has a population of 2.5 billion inhabitants. It has an average economic growth rate of 8 per cent per annum, with an average per capita income of $A7,000, equivalent to $US7,600. Many of the once endemic diseases such as malaria and smallpox have been eradicated and the continent's average population growth rate has been reduced to 1 per cent per annum and is likely to fall to 0.5 per cent by the end of the twenty-first century.

Africa today, with an expanding technological and industrial base, is no longer the economic underdog that subsisted on exports of cheap unprocessed raw materials for the economic furnaces of the so-called developed countries, but an exporter of manufactured goods that compete well on the world markets. While in the 1980s black Africa could speak of only about 1,100 tertiary education graduates per country with some countries registering as low as 300, today the ratio of technologists, scientists and medical personnel per unit population compares very well with the rest of the world.

Yes, indeed, I am proud to present to Kwame Nkrumah an Africa with political stability, strong regional co-operation and an enviable record of social justice.

But these achievements have not been painless. Looking back on the last seventy years, we see that Africa has arrived at this enviable position not without tears, blood and struggle. This is indeed a story of the triumph of the human spirit!

There have been basically five identifiable periods in this long struggle.

First was the decolonising period that lasted for a quarter of a century and saw all of Africa, except for Azania and Namibia, free. However, our founding fathers were soon to realise that Nkrumah's edict "Seek ye first the political kingdom and all shall be added unto you" was too simple. Political independence led to harsher economic dependency as commodity prices were manipulated outside Africa, not to its benefit, but to its improvement. Slowly but surely country after country fell under the yoke of economic hegemony.

Though professing non-alignment Africa was gripped in the dichotomy of the leftist socialist ideologies of the east and the faceless pragmatic capitalism of the west. The damage done to the political fabric was immeasurable. Government after government fell, as military despots, blind to the real cause of the malaise, attempted surgical solutions to the economic problems through military authoritarianism. They too failed, but not before they had desecrated our sacred rivers with blood.

After that came the years between 1987 and 95 which historians now refer to as the "IMF years", when Africa, dazzled by the blinding light of independence and floundering for direction after the decolonising period, fell prey to international money-lenders. Bitter concoctions of economic medicines were brewed in Washington and forced down the throats of the hapless African leaders. But such remedies were designed only to keep the patient a patient. Emaciated by the debt repayment syndrome and suffering from further secondary complications called "food riots", countries collapsed, and so did the era of the IMF. Then came the period between 1995-2015 when African nations were abandoned, as it were, to their own destiny by the industrial north and were thus forced to look inwards for their material and other needs. This was the beginning of the African renaissance, a period in which Africans regained their faith in themselves and their ability to charter their own destiny without voluminous recommendations from the World Bank.

The next period 2015-20 were the years of political and economic consolidation. New political groupings arose, new industrial regions developed, new resources were discovered and developed and new economic structures created. While in our fathers' era the United States dollar was the economic Medusa of the developing world, now, like South America and East Asia, we deal in our own continental currency, the African dollar (A$).

Let us now take a closer look at the various dimensions of our development in the last seventy years, from 1987 and 2057.

Environmental Cancer

Although historical climatic studies show that periodic droughts have occurred in Africa over the last two million years, a close examination of data from the middle of the last century shows that a number of anthropogenic factors seem to have led to climatic and environmental changes inimical to sustained development based on peasant technological strategies.

While the early years following the holocaust of the Second World War were full of dreams of great technological advances, these hopes soon faded as the "appropriate technology" lobbyists from the north effectively smothered any attempts by Africans to acquire advanced agricultural and manufacturing technologies. This was largely achieved by "aid" programmes in which the targets set were different from the African aspirations. Thus, for example, while an arid country like Egypt, with extremely limited arable land and water resources, was able to produce a grain harvest of up to 3 million tonnes per annum at an average yield of 4 tonnes per hectare using advanced agricultural technology, aid programmes in sub-Saharan Africa were advising methods that would yield less than 1 tonne per hectare. Thus the later twentieth century saw Africa technologically unprepared for new challenges wrought by a set of circumstances that led to new climatic patterns for which the traditional agricultural methods were no longer appropriate. The crop varieties which the Africans had cultivated for nearly half a millennium were not capable of growing in the more xeric conditions that followed the climatic shift which started in the middle of the century. Yet due to suppression of technological development, Africans were unable to adapt their agriculture and economic structures to the altered climatic conditions.

The factors that led to the climatic and environmental changes began in the middle of the century and lasted to the year 2000.

- Population growth rates that exceed resource development rates
- Livestock numbers that exceed carrying capacity on peasant range management techniques
- Deforestation in demand of:
    fuel wood
    more crop land
    commercial timber
- Soil erosion and siltation of waterways
- Loss of soil fertility
- Increase in atmospheric carbon-dioxide due to the burning of fossil fuel
- Depletion of the ozone layer due to industrial emission and forest fire.

The evidence for these factors have been presented in a number of studies. Early warnings of the impending climatic disaster are given in the studies carried out by the climate group of Goddard Space Institute. Although organizations such as The Club of Rome and the "Beyond Hunger Project" that was initiated as a result of the massive famine of the early 80s attempted to give maximum publicity to the ecological dilemmas ahead, these largely remained voices in the wilderness, as African governments were engrossed in a welter of undirectional short-term measures to cater for famine episodes and increasing economic distress.

In summary, the development was as follows:

The industrialization of the north and the increase in forest fire in Africa contributed to the alteration of the chemical composition of the atmosphere. There changes resulted in the development of a phenomenon that came to be known as the greenhouse effect and in the reduction in the ozone content of the atmosphere. Back simulation studies show changes in global climate resulting from the greenhouse effect. By the turn of the century, the mean temperature rose by between 1.5 and 3 degrees centigrade. By 2020 the mean temperature of Africa rose by as much as 5-6 degrees celsius in the arid zones and about 4 degrees celsius in the semi-arid zones. Consequently, there was an expansion of arid areas particularly in the Sahel, Southern Africa and the Horn of Africa.

In the meantime, in the period 1980 to 2000, large scale deforestation had converted areas of tropical Africa from forested woodland to overgrazed grass savanna or rainfed crop lands with a high albedo factor. By 2000 the humid forest was completely depleted in Côte d'Ivoire, Nigeria, Rwanda. Burundi, Gambia, Liberia and Madagascar, and severely reduced in the Congo Basin. In these countries, depletion rates of closed forest varied between 2 per cent to 10 per cent per annum. Daily the forests were robbed of millions of growth years and trees that had taken decades to mature were felled without replacement.

The combination of increased temperatures, increased albedo in the savanna belts and the depletion of humid rain forests resulted in increased aridity in the Sahelian and Sudan savannas. The Worldwatch Institute showed that crop production in Africa, which had shown signs of growth in the era following the Second World War, began a steady decline in the 1960s. About thirty years later crop failures became the order of the day, and came to be accepted by the ruling cliques as the inevitable lot of their people.

The high population growth, which averaged 3 per cent in the period up to 2000, resulted in the enlistment of more marginal land for crop production. On the employment market this population growth was equivalent to a job creation need of some 20 million new jobs per year. By the year 2000 all potential agricultural land reserves had been exhausted. Although the elimination of the tropical savanna woodland fly *Glossina* and *Onchocerciasis* released more ranchland, the resultant benefits were short-lived as such lands were soon converted to crop lands, with growing livestock populations being increasingly confined to diminishing grazing areas.

This high pressure on the land resulted in a dramatic increase in soil erosion, which rose from a mean of 5 tonnes per hectare per year to over 100 tonnes in the southern, eastern and west African savannas. Sediment cores from the Ethiopian highland lakes show that while in previous millennia sedimentation rates were of the order of centimetres per thousands of years, in the period between the years 2020 and 2030 the sediment accumulation was in terms of several metres per decade, indicating erosion rates of hundreds of tonnes per hectare in these once fertile humid highlands. In Madagascar the disappearance of the forest caused such erosion rates that the Madagascar Channel became known as the southern Red Sea!

The alteration of catchment morphology led to changes in hydrological parameters, with reduced ground water recharge, peaked hydrographs and frequent flooding in the lowlands. Due to the altered hydroclimatic environment there was a significant change in the agroclimatic regimes. Soil moisture rapidly declined in between rain episodes thus creating yet another source of stress for traditional crops.

The combination of poor, eroded soils, high temperatures and altered agroclimatic factors caused a more or less permanent situation of food deficit. While in the late 1950s crop production had risen to subsistence levels, a decade later crop production began to fall below subsistence and continued to decline at an average rate of 4.0 per cent between the mid-sixties and the year 2000. In contrast, population growth rates reached their peak in the period between 1970 and 1995. The demographic transition that had occurred in Asia during the same period had failed in Africa. The green revolution of Asia was echoed by famine refrains in Africa.

High silt load resulted in massive silting dams, thus impairing hydroelectric generation and water storage for city supplies. The average life expectancy of medium size to small farm dams had been reduced to less than 10 years by the year 2000.

By the year 2000, cities of the semi-arid regions were faced with periodic water shortages. Water had to be rationed to a few litres per day per household. Sanitation standards declined, resulting in periodic outbreaks of enteric diseases, such as cholera.

Frequent crop failures, water shortage, decreased agricultural output and the limited supply of natural energy led to declining economies, political instability, inter-territorial disputes for water resources, increased infant mortality, an increased number of displaced persons and the general breakdown of infrastructural facilities, while attempts by the African leaders to comply with the IMF conditions progressively alienated them from their people and severely damaged their economies.

The environmental degradation that started in the middle of the previous century and gathered momentum in the last 20 years of that century did not go unnoticed. There were periodic international forums, a plethora of regional programmes, national policies and a host of other contributions towards addressing the malaise.

However, these efforts were invariably exogenously initiated. Many industrialised world scientists became overnight "experts" on the "African Crisis", directing all programmes towards recovery to their financial advantage and constantly confounding the political leadership by their ill-informed advice.

Reconstruction and Recovery

The turn of the century saw the birth of a new citizenry, a generation to whom the words "colonialism, struggle for independence" no longer had the ring of the clarion call so familiar to their progenitors.

The era also saw the rise of a new breed of economists, no longer blinkered by the London School of Economics models and perspectives, economists who realised the enormous potential of economic energy bound in the so-called "informal sector" (an acronym for "what the London School of Economics did not teach us about"), economists who saw the futility of constructing economic models based on tax systems in which the taxable base was miniscule.

In the period prior to 2000, the question of present land tenure had been as unresolved as when the colonial powers left Africa. In this amorphus system, new pasture management and conservation measures were not possible, although much talked about. In the era after the year 2000 peasant land tenure became more formalized. Peasant agriculture became increasingly recognized in economic planning. Marketing procedures

THE BIG LIFT: A REPORT TO THE OAU 119

were extended to what was formally ignored as the informal sector with no market laws. Peasant livestock holdings that were traditionally dormant investments were mobilised into the cash economy, thus alleviating the chronic protein deficiency.

The end of the twentieth century also saw the untying of Africa from the economic apron-strings of the West. The World Bank, IMF, etc. no longer found it profitable to do business with a debt-ridden Africa. Furthermore, the development of substitutes for the raw products that Europe, America and Japan imported from Africa further eroded the African economic base. The copper of Zambia, the chrome of Zimbabwe and the bauxite of Ghana suddenly became worthless on the world commodity market.

Consequently, the new breed of African leaders sought deliverance in their local resources. New economic entities and monetary systems were formed. African scholars were charged to master the ship of African destiny. They brought to bear the power of technologies wrought and forged in the African fire: in agriculture, genetics, industrial technology, economics, informatics, the humanities and conservation.

Reforms in the status of women and a number of new services, such as child care and family planning centres coupled with extension services, freed women from restrictive household chores and enabled them to devote more time and energy to land care at a higher technological level. Research in agricultural engineering produced a new generation of implements for use by women peasant farmers.

These reforms had a tremendous effect on the job seeking habits of the men. Fear of being landless and unemployed in the city drove many young men back to the land to secure their tenure. This back migration to the rural areas had a significant effect on the labour situation in the peasant farming sector. Furthermore, these young farmers, with their entrepreneurship, were quick to take advantage of the technological innovations that were coming out of the research centres. Thus peasant agriculture was transformed from being an unpleasant occupation of the less enterprising sector of the population to a rural profession with a tremendous drive.

The most dramatic event that led to the recovery of Africa was the launching of "Africa Woman", the environmental measuring satellite built jointly by Chinese and African engineers. Coupled with the development of computer manufacturing capabilities in Azania the African capability at environmental management was greatly increased. Using satellite data, forestry and environmental scientists are now capable of planning reclamation programmes with great predictive precision. Furthermore, the increased earnings of the peasant farmer, and thus his access to other forms of energy, has enabled a change in life-style which has resulted in the reduction of woodfuel demand. Tillage and micro-irrigation systems, developed at the Zimbabwe Institute of Agricultural Engineering and Environmental Management, have resulted in a tremendous reduction in erosion. Consequently, our rivers, which for decades have looked like weathered skeletons, now flow once again with waters of blessing.

The turnabout in the African economic situation occurred in the year 2025. You will recall that the period 1987 to the year 2000 was marked by economic deterioration. In the circumstances, African economies experienced an average annual decline in per capita economic growth of the order of 1 per cent in this period.

The ensuing period of twenty-five years was marked by considerable soul-searching, objective analysis and the generation of rational economic policies addressing themselves to the true origins of the African development crisis. I am pleased to report that the turnabout in our economic policies and outlook was engineered primarily by our leaders, social scientists and thinkers, many of whom had returned from exile. In these years the leadership have learnt that letting our intellectuals speak is better than locking them up.

The African economic crisis was brought to a head by the APPER (The African Provisional Programme for Economic Recovery) agreement of 1986 in which African leaders virtually mandated Africa to the international money-lenders through the UN. This agreement, however, helped to sharpen the lack of faith African leaders had in the abilities of their own technocrats. It was the abhorrence of African scholars to the agreement that gave rise to the African renaissance movement. African intellectuals had been humiliated to the lowest status. Failure after failure, crisis after crisis later confirmed the apprehensions of the African intellectuals about neo-colonially manipulated capitalism or doctrinaire socialism from above.

The renaissance led to re-evaluating the concept of "difference". Differences were seen as not necessarily bad. People did not need to

THE BIG LIFT: A REPORT TO THE OAU 121

be dictated to or forced into brutal uniformity in the name of development. The movement led to the realisation that local, national, and subregional efforts could only be promoted in a spirit of self-reliance, interdependency and democracy. The African scientists, who had largely worked in isolation, began to regroup and formulate regional concepts in the management of natural resources, trade and commerce, social services and cultural development.

There were sweeping continent-wide agrarian reforms in which the peasant farmer was no longer relegated to the so-called informal sector. New concepts in agricultural economics resulted in farmers receiving realistic prices and, after a faltering start in the stabilisation period (2000-2025), productivity rose twentyfold between 2025 and 2057. Considerable credit for this must be given to the African governments which have shifted greater shares of their budgets to agricultural research, extension services and rural infrastructure, and de-escalated the military expenditure spiral which characterized the turbulent years.

In particular, there has been greater emphasis on agricultural sciences, especially in bio-technological innovations in food production. We did away with state policies which subsidized urban consumers and penalised agricultural producers. We adopted realistic exchange rate policies which eventually led to the consolidation of exchange rates in the "Afran", the continental currency unit of the African Development Bank. Over the years, these policies have stimulated demand for local consumer goods and catalysed indigenous industrial production.

The recovery of the African economy attracted back international business concerns, but this time on an equal partner basis. The international community recognised new opportunities for investment and business partnerships. External concessional lending to Africa rose tenfold in real terms after the year 2000 and debt relief was accorded to our states on the basis of their capacity to institute production-oriented stabilisation programmes. This, as ministers may recall, was part of the Mandela plan for Africa's economic recovery, which was based on the Marshall plan of past years. I wish to take this opportunity to thank those of Africa's friends who heeded her in her hour of need.

The pace of faster growth and incomes has induced a decline in fertility rates and a slow-down in the population growth rate of Africa. From the heights of 2.7 per cent in the closing years of the last century,

the rate fell to 2 per cent in 2025 and is now estimated at 1 per cent.
The terms of trade for primary commodities produced by Africa improved after 2025 after a phenomenal decline. This followed the industrial crisis in the Western world which was induced by raw material substitutes and new markets for our agricultural commodities in the newly industrialised states of Asia, Africa and Latin America. This enabled us to expand our industrial base beginning from the production of consumer goods to the point where many states are now producing capital goods for the African market.

In the wake of the climatic changes in the northern hemisphere, which in the first half of the twenty-first century left it both less productive in agriculture and generally less habitable, African states have risen to the challenges and discharged their international responsibilities with dignity and honour. In 2053, the Southern African Economic Community dispatched 20,000 tonnes of grain to Britain and Ireland, the most affected countries.

African economists and statesmen have pioneered the "mutual assistance programme in food-aid", an international food security insurance system in which affected countries draw from an insurance fund without the stigma which was associated with the "famine relief" food handouts of the late twentieth century. The system was derived from African traditional economic systems and our notions of extended family responsibilities. We have therefore bequeathed to the world the economic model known as "no starvation ever in a world of surplus food", which has become the standard platform of the world community.

In a sense, Honourable Ministers, Africa has done its share in reducing global tensions and in eliminating in our century the prospects of mass hunger and the old humiliation of hungry people scrounging for food aid.

Political Renewal

During the past thirty years, we can truly say that Africa has developed politically. We all recall the era of constant coups d'état, conflicts, wars, and political assassinations.

The Organization of African Unity adopted a Human Rights Charter in 1983 at the Nairobi OAU Summit. Most states only paid lip service to it until the terribly dark era of the 1990s brought Africa to a full awareness with regard to human rights and the process of democratization.

In Africa today, democracy has taken different forms according to different cultural, historical and socio-economic conditions. Power is transferred constitutionally. No state exists in Africa today that does not have at least one party (and all one-party states allow for democratic multi-candidate elections), and several autonomous associations including grassroot and national voluntary development organizations. Professional associations and all other civic associations have provided an excellent training ground for future local, national or even regional leadership. Today, we are proud to say that the majority of African leaders (heads of state, cabinet ministers) are former leaders of various civil society associations; and only about a third of the continent's leadership group comes from other national institutions such as the armed forces, with another third from the commercial sector.

The attainment of political stability, matured leadership with proven records of experience, knowledge and service, has facilitated toleration and the implementation of human rights. Consequently the United Nations High Commission for Refugees in Africa is now primarily occupied with resettling victims of natural disasters from other parts of the world.

During the period 1957-2000, most of Africa's highly trained work force felt it difficult, if not impossible, to work in their own home countries. Democratization, and implementation of the OAU's Human Rights Charter has finally allowed Africa's scientists, social scientists and artists to serve their own peoples, thereby contributing to the remarkable period of recovery, renewal and reconstruction that we have witnessed.

Political developments internally were helped and strengthened by inter-African political, socio-cultural and economic developments. The OAU, as noted, is as strong as the member states that constitute it. We all recall how weak and paralysed the OAU has been. Nevertheless, it was the OAU that catalysed the Lagos Plan of Action and the special United Nations session on Africa and Charter of Human Rights. The OAU had also facilitated various Pan-African umbrella associations such as those for African trade unions, youth and students, co-operatives, professional associations and commercial groups.

During the period of economic stagnation and decline, African states were virtually bankrupt. State services deteriorated and the people withdrew into what was generally referred to as informal economics. Among the various responses to this challenge was the formation of viable indigenous grassroots associations to facilitate production and provide services. Extension service agents became part and parcel of local community groups rather than individuals parachuted from the outside, receiving salaries from capital cities or even from the outside. Grassroots organizations (GRO's) sprang up everywhere; even the poor in the deteriorating cities began to organize themselves into local self-help, self-reliant groups. External international NGOs (Non-Governmental Organizations) helped in this process especially during the period 1974-1990 when drought and refugee crises led many of them to raise funds in order to provide humanitarian relief to African communities.

One year after the special United Nations session on the African crisis, the Forum for African Voluntary Organizations (FAVO) was launched in Dakar, Senegal (May 30, 1987), in a move to strengthen Pan-Africanism.

African scientists grouped into the African Academy of Sciences have continued to contribute actively to reflection, research and development of scientific thought and practice in the Third World.

African leaders and technocrats began, as a result of the serious calamities of the 1987-2000 period, to exert greater efforts to strengthen new and existing Pan-African and subregional organizations and zones of subregional common currencies and to provide freer movement of people, currencies and technologies. In short, the OAU came to find itself mostly facilitating strongly functional subregional groups.

Such subregional bodies now cover:

a   emergency contingency plans
b   early warning systems for disasters
c   subregional food security systems
d   food crop security systems
e   livestock development
f   development of fisheries in land and sea
g   energy resource development including promotion of alternative energy sources
h   water resources and development

i   range management and joint anti-desertification measures.
j   infrastructural development (roads, railways, ports, airports, telecommunications, etc.)
k   human resources development — co-ordination of training institutions and research centres for indigenous and appropriate technologies.

Strengthened subregional organizations and functioning grassroots and national level institutions helped to restore the richness of African civil societies. They also contributed to improving civil society; state, intra-state and inter-state relations allowed Africa to deal realistically and democratically with issues of ethnic, linguistic and cultural diversity and thus resolve national problems in such a way that colonially inherited borders no longer provided serious constraints to the natural, ecological and economic movement of people, goods and vital services. This provides the key to understanding the rapid progress attained during the past thirty years.

Cultural Renaissance

The growth of regional economic groupings resulted in the increased mobility of the African peoples. While in the twentieth century African capitals were connected through Paris and London, the eve of the twenty-first century saw inter-African communications much improved. This has had a melting effect on regional cultural groups that had hitherto been isolated by the intra-African travel barriers so characteristic of the previous century. Consequently common language groups have emerged in various parts of Africa. (Swahili is now a world language taught even in Japan.) This cultural coalescence has enabled Africans to identify more with each other than with their former colonial masters. No longer is Africa divided into Anglophone and Francophone groups, but into regional language blocs equivalent to the Germanic and Romance language blocs of Europe.

Religion continued to sustain African life, African family and social life during the calamities of drought and wars, our natural and man-made disasters. The AIDS epidemic strengthened the African tendency to seek moral renewal through spiritual visions. The religious and moral re-awakening strengthened the issue of quality in leadership and facilitated the decline of corruption and related malpractices. It also checked the tendencies towards total societal breakdown and helped to stop African decline just as it reached the point of no return.

Nevertheless, religious renewals did lead to religious conflicts waged by fringes of religious fanatics. Through painful periods of trial and error, African religious policies have evolved and may be summed up as thus:

a   All African states have adopted secular constitutional policies;
b   Freedom of religious belief; even individual non-belief is tolerated and respected;
c   All religions are equally respected;
d   External evangelical missions have been phased out;
e   African traditional religions have been accorded equal respect and honour beside the various adaptations of Islam and Christianity.

Religion continues to play a vital role in civil society, in civic associations, in PVOs inspired by humanitarian religious visions. Like languages, African religions as well as the adapted international ones have come to play a positive role in strengthening indigenous institutions in that they promote self-reliance and good leadership and facilitate unity in diversity.

Changes in Southern Africa

Honourable Ministers, allow me finally to report on some of the major challenges and developments in the southern African region (specifically in the republics of Azania and Namibia) that have captured the world's attention and occupied the energies of our Organization of African Unity over the last seventy years.

At the time of the General Assembly's Special Session on the Social and Economic Crisis in Africa of 1986, calls were being made by African governments to apply mandatory and comprehensive sanctions against the then white minority regime in South Africa in an effort to bring about a peaceful and negotiated end to its abhorrent system of apartheid and to its illegal occupation of Namibia in defiance of the UN Security Council Resolution No. 242. The regime had responded with intransigence, the systematic destabilization of neighbouring states through economic strangulation, military intervention and even the violent overthrow of their governments. Internally, more vicious repression took place during an almost decade-long state of emergency, accompanied by a ruthlessly reinforced information blackout, under cover of which massive and indiscriminate detentions, torture and maiming took place.

The world looked on helplessly as the situation deteriorated. In the USA, the administration elected in 1988 did not pursue the geopolitical excesses of President Reagan, but it had great difficulty in extricating itself from the doctrinaire foreign policy sharpened over the preceding two presidential terms. The situation was aggravated by protectionism and trade wars as the USA's economic empire began to crumble under assault from the new industrial power of Japan and South East Asia. Meanwhile, the other superpower of the day (USSR) had its attention focussed on its extended war of nerves with the USA over threat of a nuclear holocaust. Thus, the worsening situation in Southern Africa had failed to attract enough attention by the then "superpowers" and their allies in time to divert catastrophe.

The volatile situation, more than ever charged with latent all-out violence, was pushed in the direction of its apocalyptic climax by the death in prison of my grandfather, Nelson Mandela, who had spent only the first third of his life in freedom. The anger of the blacks turned what had hitherto been a not-so-successful guerilla war into civil war. The OAU and the United Nations Security Council intervened to avert declarations of war in the region, as the apartheid regime turned to even more vicious reprisals against the front-line states, which by then were openly harbouring recruitment and training centres for young volunteers coming from all over black Africa.

Then on Dingaan's Day, as he drove to Parliament, the President of South Africa, who had been constantly denounced by the extreme right-wing as pussy-footing with the blacks, was assassinated by a gang of white vigilantes, who, disguised as young guerillas from Soweto, rocket-bombed his motorcade with Soviet-made bazookas. The plot had been carefully engineered by some top South African army generals who wanted an excuse for an all-out onslaught on the frontline states. In a stage-managed show of frenzied anger, the South African army, which had always denied allegations that it had quietly developed nuclear capacity, responded by dropping a mini-nuclear bomb on the Angolan oil installations at Cabinda. Confronted with such a blatant challenge, the Soviets could not help but posture threats of retaliation in similar kind. Faced with the threat of a world war and the horrors of hundreds of thousands of dying and maimed people in Zaire, Congo and Angola, the world community finally reacted quickly and the now historical combined United Nations Security Council/General Assembly session took place in June 2000. Joint OAU/UN peace-keeping forces were quickly dispatched to the region.

United Nations-supervised elections were held in Namibia, and the People's Republic of Namibia under the SWAPO-led government took its place as a sovereign state among the community of nations in June 2002.

Meanwhile in South Africa the process of negotiations to secure safeguard for racial minorities under Black majority rule and dismantle the Bantustans was long-drawn-out; the rehabilitation of hundreds of thousands from war and exile and preparations for the twenty million eligible Blacks to participate in elections for the first time were time-consuming endeavours. Finally, one person-one vote elections were held in January 2005, an ANC-led government of national unity was sworn in and the Democratic Republic of Azania was born in June 2005.

As was to be expected, the White backlash as a result of the ANC electoral victory was as vicious as the reactionaries had threatened. On the one hand, misguided professionals emigrated en masse to Australia, New Zealand, Latin America and even to some of the Pacific islands where struggles by indigenous populations for self-determination had suffered an all-time setback when in 1990 the French white settlers in New Caledonia declared unilateral independence, and the French government proceeded to reach a settlement with them restoring the status quo ante. On the other hand, hysteria produced comic situations as the forces of reaction turned on themselves tactics previously reserved for blacks. "Whiteystan" is the only way to describe the attempted secession of the Orange Free State and the internal exodus as whites tried to settle there. Then bands of white rogues went underground to commit acts of economic sabotage geared at encouraging disinvestment and discouraging foreign investors.

During the initial period of ten years or so, the new governments in southern Africa were therefore occupied in not only resolving a multitude of internal problems (such as, the social reintegration of the victims of apartheid and liberation struggles, the construction of majority-oriented educational systems and the rehabilitation of agriculture), but also in generally dismantling the labyrinth of the rules and regulations of apartheid, while taking care to reassure minorities. This has been largely achieved, helped by the positive attitude of the big industrial powers of Brazil, India and the Association of South East Asian Nations, as well as the solidarity of the Blacks of the United States and Canada.

Further, in recognition of the crucial and multiple roles played by women in the protracted war of liberation, the region as a whole has taken the lead in instituting programmes and progressive legislation in favour of widows, woman-headed households and women in general. Although the policy of appointing women to at least a half of the cabinet and the higher echelons of public service, for which valiant women politicians and activists have been fighting, has yet to be implemented in full, the fact that the policy now exists is a sign that we can look forward to a future characterized by true gender equality in both privileges and responsibility.

Developments in the last twenty-five years have concretely demonstrated the potential for collective self-reliance in Africa as Azania and Namibia started to play a more active role within the regional cooperation framework and, as their mineral resources and Azania's technological advance have progressively become opened up, the two countries have engineered exchanges with the rest of Africa. Indeed, one can say that Africa's "Big Lift" would not have been possible in the short term without the "Big Push" from southern Africa.

At the political level, the region has given concrete demonstration of the Pan-Africanist ideal by initiating popular debate, referendums and negotiations on confederal arrangements involving Azania, Namibia, the small enclave countries of Lesotho and Swaziland, as well as Botwana, all of which share not only common borders but identical cultures and languages. I can just see the ghost of Kwame Nkrumah, the father of Pan-Africanism, looking at these happenings with an inscrutable smile.

Honourable Ministers, it is on a note of triumph that I close my report to your august assembly. Considering the gloom that reigned in this particular region just a century ago, with all the countries in the region under the crippling yoke of colonial rule, its progress is truly remarkable. Africa has risen from her ashes.... Africa has redeemed herself. Kwame's spirit lives yet.

8

Conclusions: Levers of Change and Implications for Research and Policy

Africa's Future Workshop—the construction of alternative scenarios, the writing of future histories—is a renewed appraisal of African potential and a fresh vision of African possiblities. How might such an African vision actually come about in the mid twenty-first century? By way of a very tentative answer, the workshop undertook two tasks. The first was to analyze the four future histories for their implicit or explicit explanations of how the Big Lift was realized. The second was the identification of a set of research topics, reflecting the issues raised in the histories and exploring, in particular, the levers of change.

Implicit in most, and explicit in several of the future histories are seven promising levers of change:

- A salutory but unintentional delinkage of the African economies may take place through both the current economic difficulties and reduced international interest in primary products.
- The liberation of Southern Africa may provide a new source of capital and energy for all of Africa.
- The struggle to liberate African men and women and to restore their cultural heritage may lead to the utilization of the neglected potentials of great sectors of society: women, intellectuals, and ethnic groups presently excluded or ignored.
- Population growth, while initially difficult, can in the long run provide new incentives for development, new energy in numbers and youth, and new markets for interregional trade.
- More responsive and accountable governments, organized in broader regional units and novel forms of Pan-African unity can provide fresh leadership.
- New efforts of science and technological innovation can utilize both high technology and grassroots activity and emphasize such areas as linguistics, natural products, and social organizations.

Economic Delinkage

Advocates of alternative policies for African nations have pursued directions of greater economic independence, rejection of neo-colonialism, and self-reliance. Such policies emphasize the delinkage of African economics from the strong connections with global markets and monetary standards and the development of regional industries and markets. Three of the future histories specifically foresee such delinkage, in the words of one: "delinkage by default." The circumstances of the defaults differ. They include: the failure to meet International Monetary Fund requirements; an inability to pay debts; a fatigue on the part of donors with recurrent African crises; and a loss of primary commodity markets, as new biotechnological innovations make developed countries less dependent on tropical sources of commodities such as cocoa, coffee, sugar, and tea. This delinkage by default, while initially aggravating the economic malaise, gradually provides both space and incentive for local initiatives, for regional industries, and for African-based markets.

Liberation of Southern Africa

In the future histories of Africa, the liberation of South Africa and Namibia does not come easily or early, taking until 1995 in one history and 2002 in another. But both the struggle itself and the highly industrialized economy the victor inherits, adds new elements to African potential. In the course of the struggle, the frontline states link their own economies closer. These in turn link to the rich potential of South Africa's economy with its enormous mineral wealth, developed industry, and important technological skills and human resources.

Cultural Liberation

The deeper and in some ways more difficult struggle for cultural freedom parallels the liberation struggle. This effort to maintain and to reclaim Africa's cultural heritage is found in all the future histories. The details differ, but there is emphasis on the maintenance and use of local

CONCLUSIONS: LEVERS OF CHANGE   133

languages, on traditional religion, and on family and clan social organization. In the course of such effort new and surprising opportunities emerge to build upon traditional forms. For example, one history projects African oral tradition and multilingualism as a base for the development of systems of informatics innovation and the maintenance and use of multiple traditional languages. Still another sees potential for a new form of corporate capitalism based on clan and extended family relationships. And all report new energy, pride, and self-sufficiency in the course of such a struggle.

Related to this cultural development as well as political change is the realization of the potential of three great sectors of society presently under-utilized: women, excluded ethnic groups, and indigenous intellectuals. The future histories speak of greater utilization of the agricultural, organizational, and entrepreneurial skills of women, the entrance of ethnic groups into areas of national life from which they are currently excluded, and a greater appreciation and utilization of local scientists as well as a growing toleration of intellectual criticism.

Population Growth

The Big Lift scenario projects a 2057 population for Africa of 2.5 billion people, larger than that of the Current Perspective. The future histories acknowledge the difficulties brought about by such rapid population growth as more than five-fold. But at least two of the histories stress the stimulus value of higher population densities. For one, there is the observable relationship between higher population densities and agricultural intensification. In this formulation, which draws on work by Ester Boserup, societies undertake to use intensified means of production under the spur of increased population. For another, there is the requirement of significant population densities to make feasible electric power grids, improved transport networks, and industrial and commercial markets.

State Renewal and Unity

African traditions have always emphasized leadership, an emphasis that has failed Africa in its translation into modern independent states. All the future histories painfully recount this bitter and continuing history of failure to institutionalize the democratic process while over-bureaucratizing government. But all of the future histories project a more democratic Africa, with civil government, tolerance, and respect for human rights. Several emphasize multi-party systems.

Two main forces move along the pathway to renewed government, one from below, and one from a wider community. In several of the future histories, social movements (religious, mutual support groups, co-operatives, and other non-governmental organizations) emerge to fill the space left by the collapse of state structures. The sheer number and diversity of these organizations and their mutual accommodation provides alternative opportunities for leadership beyond the military organizations, the political party, or the civil service.

At the same time the larger economic and political pressures make regional groups and Pan-African unity more of a necessity than a simple idea. The delinkage by default encourages the development of larger internal African markets. The struggle of Southern Africa creates new regional unity in the south. And the cultural liberation increases interest in the commonality of African cultures as well as their diversity. In several future histories, common regional languages emerge hand in hand with common currencies.

Science and Technology

In general, all the histories project an African future with high technology, though they differ on the transition events that they emphasize and the role for so-called appropriate technology. All emphasize greater reliance on indigenous scientific expertise, partly aided by the delinkage of economies with the international economic order or by the growth of grassroots alternatives. One history emphasizes the role of appropriate technology transfers from Asian and Latin American Third World countries. Several emphasize "appropriate" high technology. Examples cited are: an agrobiotechnology emphasizing fermentation processes, superconductivity making feasible the use of dispersed hydroelectric sources, information sciences building on cultural traditions of language, oral history, and parapsychology. Or simply put, a science and technology with an African face.

Resources and Environment

Several future histories emphasize the under-explored and under-utilized land, energy, and mineral resources of Africa. The conquest of the tsetse fly and the proper management of tropical soils will make available large new sources of productive land. Major oil and other mineral finds are confidently projected for the future, coming on line coincident with a renewed energy crisis in the industrialized world. A denser population grid will be able to utilize the substantial but scattered hydro-electric wealth. And in two of the histories, the global climatic change from increased greenhouse effects enhances the comparative advantage of Africa's climate by adding moisture to currently semi-arid regions, while diminishing moisture in some of the northern hemisphere grain belts.

Common Characteristics

These major levers of change have a common characteristic. They invoke surprising but favourable outcomes from trends viewed unfavourably or ignored by the current perspective. For example, the current perspective sees in economic delinkage — a loss of external support; in traditional languages, religion, and social organization — backwardness; in liberation struggles — bloodshed and suffering; in population growth — an enlarged burden on fragile societies; in Pan-African unity — continued failure; and in climate change — increased potential for drought and desertification. The future histories do not ignore these negative trends, but view them in dialectical fashion as creating contradictions, perhaps negative in the short-run but with surprising promise for the long-run.

Of course, no-one can tell what the actual levers of change will be in Africa's future history. These are exemplary, illustrative of the kinds of forces that could power change in the future. But they are more than examples, they are possibilities as well. They are worth exploring as such and each has led to the identification of one or more topics for future research:

Proposed Research Topics

- *The new Pan-Africanism: regional co-operation through parallel markets*
- *The new African: the Pan-Africanization of urban culture*

- *Grassroots organizations, technological innovation and democratization*
- *Intra-African migration sources of innovation through religious movements*
- *African languages in the context of expanding intra-African interaction*
- *Relationship between African universities, research institutes and grassroots organizations/community development*
- *Population growth and agricultural change in densely populated areas of Africa*
- *Culture and personality in Africa*
- *Resource conservation in land-abundant areas in Africa*
- *Informatics in relation to language and non-formal education*
- *Informal spread of high technology in Africa*
- *Biotechnology and Africa's genetic heritage*
- *Impact of climatic changes on African development in the next century*
- *The gender issue and Africa's future development process*
- *The Lagos Plan of Action and the new social movements*
- *Social and scientific responses to epidemics in Africa*
- *African life-styles*
- *Symbolic culture and its implications for development (e.g. in the areas of personality: cognitive psychology, psychiatry, imagination, etc)*
- *Alternative methods of predicting the future*

APPENDIX

Participants in the Beyond Hunger Project

Professor Chinua Achebe
Department of English
University of Nigeria
Nsukka, NIGERIA
Telex: 51440 ASUTEC NG

Dr Hussein M. Adam
Senior Research Associate
International Relief/Development Project
Harvard University
Graduate School of Education
Longfellow Hall, Appian Way
Cambridge, MA 02138 USA

Professor Deborah E. Ajakaiye
Dean, Faculty of Natural Sciences
University of Jos, NIGERIA
Tel: (off) 073-55935 X263;
(res) 073-52910; Telex: 81136

Dr Dianzungu Dia Biniakunu
Universite Marien Ngouabi
B.P. 237
Brazzaville
REPUBLIQUE POPULAIRE DU CONGO

Professor Michael Chege
Institute of Developmental Studies
University of Nairobi
P.O. Box 30197
Nairobi, KENYA

Professor Goran Hyden
Department of Political Science
University of Florida
Gainesville, FL 32611 USA
Tel: (res) 904-375-0285; (off) 904-392-6539

Ms Rosemary Jommo
Acting Executive Secretary
AAWORD

C/o CODESRIA, BP 3304
Dakar, SENEGAL

Dr Calestous Juma
Public Law Institute
P.O. Box 69313
Nairobi, KENYA
Tel: (off) 330098 or 334529; (res) 505920

Robert W. Kates
Alan Shawn Feinstein World Hunger Program
Brown University, Box 1831
Providence, R10912 USA
Tel: 401-863-2700

Dr Kabiru Kinyanjui
Institute of Development Studies
University of Nairobi
P.O. Box 30197
Nairobi, KENYA

Dr Christopher H.D. Magadza
University Lake Kariba Research Station
P.O., Box 48
Kariba, ZIMBABWE
Tel: (off) 263-61-22312; (res) 2707

Dr Thandika Mkandawire
CODESRIA
B.P. 3304
Dakar, SENEGAL

Professor G.C.M. Mutiso
Consultant
MUTICON
Nairobi, KENYA
Tel: 747010

Professor S.O. Ojo
Department of Geography
University of Lagos
Lagos, NIGERIA

LIST OF PARTICIPANTS

Dr Achola Pala Okeyo
International Centre of Insect Physiology
and Ecology (ICIPE)
P.O. Box 30772
Nairobi, KENYA

Professor Kwesi Prah
Institute of Southern African Studies
National University of Lesotho
P.O. Roma, LESOTHO

Dr Amos Sawyer
Workshop on Political Theory and Policy Analysis
Indiana University
513 North Park Street
Bloomington, Indiana 47405, USA
Tel: 812-335-3153 or -0441

Dr Mahendra Shah
127 Dray Court Avenue
Kenton Harrow, Middlesex
ENGLAND HA3 0DA

Dr Nomtheto Simelane
Department of Political Science
University of Swaziland
Kwaluseni Campus
P.O. Kwaluseni, SWAZILAND
Tel: 84011/3

For further information about the Beyond Hunger Project write to:

Dr Achola Pala Okeyo
ICIPE
P.O. Box 30772
NAIROBI
Kenya.

In the United States:

Dr Goran Hyden
Alan Shawn Feinstein World Hunger Program
Box 1831
Brown Univesity
Providence RI 02912

Index

Acid deposition 70
Aeronautics 91
Afran 121
Africa in 2057 103 - 104
African Academy of Sciences 15, 106, 108, 124
African Agriculture: The Next 25 Years 52, 55
African Council for Advanced Science and Technology 96
African Court of Justice 96
African Development Bank 121
African dollar 114
African Human Rights Council 96
African intellectuals 83
African languages 88, 100 - 101
   ascendancy of 101
   religious movements and 100
African literature 88
African Provisional Programme for Economic Recovery 120
African renaissance 114, 126
African self-reliance 92
African vision 22, 23, 81 - 135
   and action 23
   and policy 23
   and research 23
   histories inspired by 81 - 135
African way 89
Africa's future 3, 5, 8 - 13, 16, 27 - 72, 81 - 135
   alternative image of 81 - 135
   and the Beyond Hunger Project 6, 7
   challenge of 8 - 13
   conventional image of 27 - 72
   current perspective on 3
   debate on 4
   early perspective on 3
   image of 8
   magnetic images of 5
   scholars' concern about 16
Africa's Future Workshop 131
Africa Woman 119
Africa Year 2000 14
Age structure 40
Agrarian reforms 121

Agricultural production 51 - 56
Agricultural research 121
Agriculture 8, 29, 35, 51 - 58, 92, 94, 105 - 106, 117, 118, 119, 120, 121
   and ruralization 94
   feminization of 105
   green revolution in 105 - 106, 117
   impact of drought on 105
   industrialization and 94
   irrigated 56 - 57, 58
   land tenure and 118, 119
   peasant 118, 119, 120, 121
   prospects in 51 - 58
   revolution in 92
Agriculture, Toward 2000 52, 55, 56
Agro-based industrialization 94
Agrobiotechnology 134
Agroclimatic regimes 117
Agroforestry 87
AIDS 86 - 87, 125
   and moral renewal 125
Air pollution 70
Albedo 116
All-powerful state 104
Alternative Patterns of Development and Life Styles for the Africa Region 14
Alternative vision 79 - 136
Amin, Prof. Samir 14
Angola 128
Apartheid 85, 126, 127
   abolition of 85
Arabic 100, 108
Arable land 56, 58
   and FAO data 56
Authoritarian leadership 85, 94, 99, 113
Azania 113, 126, 128, 129

Baby boom 86
Banana fermentation 110
Bauxite 119
Beyond Hunger: Africa's Future 1957-2057 Project 5 - 16, 18 - 23, 103, 115, 137 - 139
   and the intellectual community 5
   assumptions of 6

central challenge to 13
interdisciplinary nature of 14
Kericho Workshop 14, 18, 103
methodological origin of 15
methodology of 18 – 23
notion of research 7
participants in 13 – 16, 137 – 139
Big Lift 20, 79 – 130
Big Rift 20
Biogas production 66
Biological contamination 36
Biological warfare 90
Biotechnological industries 95
Biotechnology 121
Boserup, Ester 133
Brazil 90, 129
Bretton-Woods agreement 84
Brooks 11, 12
Bureaucratization 104, 134
Burkina Faso 44

Cabinda 128
Caloric supply 53
Canada 109
Capital goods 35, 50
Capitalism 113
Carbon dioxide 115
Catastrophe theories 12, 13
Catchment morphology 117
Cereal production 52, 54, 55
   self-sufficiency ratio in 52
Chad 43
Challenge of Africa 3 – 16
   conventional understanding of 3
Charcoal 64
Chemists 61
Chernobyl incident 2
Childhood dependency ratio 40
Child labour 97
China 109
Chivizi electric steel process 110
Christianity 126
Chrome 119
Civil rights violation 86
Civil society 95, 125, 126

and religion 126
   improvement of 125
Civil society associations 123
Climatic disaster 114, 115
Climatic patterns 115
Coal 62, 63, 68, 69
   demand for 68, 69
   production 63
Collective colonialism 99
Collective self-esteem 88
Colonial borders 125
Colonial rule 111
Commercial relevançe 88
Committee on African Development
   Strategies 28
Common currencies 88
Common monetary systems 88
Concessionary lending 121
Consolidation 92, 94
Contradictions 83
Conventional wisdom 8, 18, 19, 21, 22,
   36 – 41, 103, 112
   against alternative futures 22
   as surprise free 10, 18
   indicators 18, 27, 29
Cooperatives 87
Copper 119
Cost of progress 89, 90, 92, 113
Council for Development of Economic
   and Social Research in Africa
   (CODESRIA) 14, 15, 16
Council of Foreign Relations 4
Crisis perspective 3, 5, 13, 28, 30
Crop failures 116
Crude death rate 43
Culturalized science 97
Cultural liberation 132 – 133
Cultural renaissance 85, 89, 125 – 126,
   132 – 133
Cultural revolution 85, 89, 125 – 126,
   132 – 133
Cultural trends 101 – 102
Culture 6, 19, 33
   as catalyst for change 6
Current perspectives 18, 19, 27 – 72
   and tunnel vision 33

INDEX 143

limitation of 30

Dams 117
Dance 102
Debates 6, 7, 16
  need for 6, 7
  role of Beyond Hunger Project in 16
Debt burden 84
Debt relief 121
Debt repayment syndrome 114
Deforestation 29, 35, 62, 69, 70, 115, 116
Degradation of women 97, 98
  and tourism 98
Dehumanization 95
Deindustrialization 93, 94
Delinking by default 85, 87, 131, 132
Democracy 87, 92, 96
Democratic struggle 95
Democratization 95, 98, 123, 134
  and women's emancipation 98
Demographic expansion 84
Demographic expectations 36 – 45
Demographic projections 18 – 19, 33
Demographic transition 29, 42
Demographic variables 31, 34
Dependency theory 20
Desertification 29, 35, 62, 70
  and cattle grazing 70
Deterioration 3
Development 3, 9
  as a push-pull process 9
Dialectic movement 22
Dictatorship 87
Difference 120 – 121
Dingaan's Day 127
Discontinuities 12
Domestic capacity 4, 5
Driving myth 87
Drought 83, 105, 114

Economic Community of West African States (ECOWAS) 87
Economic cooperation and development 27, 49

Economic dependence 113
Economic hegemony 113
Economic performance 28, 45 – 51
  as source of pessimism 45
Economic Summit, 1980 14
Economic trends 93 – 94
Economic turnabout 120
Economic variables 31, 34
Economy 8
Edmonds 67
Education 58 – 59, 105
Egypt 114
Energy 8, 31, 62 – 69, 88
  consumption 66 – 68
  development, 2020 57, 97
  growth of production 62
  in the 21st century 88
  non-renewable 62 – 63
  oil and natural gas 62
  projections of supply and demand 68 – 69
Energy consumption 66 – 68
  agriculture and 67
  place of oil in 67
  transportation and 67
Energy resources 88
Engineers 60, 61
English language 100, 101, 108
Enteric diseases 118
Environment 135
Environmental cancer 114
Environmental degradation 28, 29
Environmental management 120
Environmental trends 69 – 70
Environmental variables 31, 34
Epidemics 86
Ethiopia 117
Ethnic-religious conflicts 99
Euphoria 19, 29, 30, 83, 104
  and Nkrumah 83
  between 1950 and 1970 104
Evolutionary paradigm 11
Exchange rate 46
Export economy 85
Extended family 89, 133
Extension services 121

Extrapolation 18, 22

Family stress 97
Famines 13, 30, 116, 117
FAO Atlas on African Agriculture 112
Federation of East Africa 91
Feminist movement 97
Feminization of agriculture 105
Fertiliser consumption 56
Fertility 41 - 43
  in Kenya 42, 44
  projected rates 42
Flooding 117
Food and Agriculture Organization 18, 52, 55
Food consumption 51 - 52
Food deficit 117
Food imports 12, 105
Food production 29, 31, 35
Food riots 114
Food sufficiency 91, 112
Food supplies 52
  projections for 52
Food surplus 107
Ford Foundation 16
Formal education 105
Forum for African Voluntary Organizations 124
Fossil fuel 61, 62
French language 100, 101, 108
Fuelwood energy 64, 65
Fundamentalist movements 99
Future 10, 11
Future histories 21, 79 - 130
Future scenarios 5, 8, 20
Futures science 11

Gender issue 89, 97 - 98
Geothermal energy 64, 88
Ghana 111, 119
Glassroot organizations 124, 136
Global 2000 52, 54
Glossina 116
Goddard Space Institute 115
Greece 33, 34

compared to Africa in future 33, 34
Green-house effect 109, 116
Green revolution 105 - 106, 117
Gross Domestic Product 27, 28 - 29, 31, 34, 36, 46, 47, 51, 55, 59
  and education expenditure 59
  projected per capita 46, 48, 49
Gross production 46 - 49
Groundwater depletion 70
Grouping of River Organizations in West Africa (GROW) 87, 88

Hausa 101, 108
Heavy metal contamination 70
High technology industries 91, 97
Holling, C.S. 11
Honeymoon 83
Hunger 5, 116, 122
Human resources 8, 56 - 61
Human resource variables 31, 34, 58 - 61
Human rights 92, 95, 108, 123, 134
  violation of 95
Human Rights Charter, 1983 122, 123
Hyden, Goran 15
Hydroclimatic environment 117
Hydroelectric power 63-64, 88, 117
Hydrological parameters 117

Image of Africa 5, 20
  and non-Africans 20
Imaging 18, 21
IMF years 92, 105, 113
Independence 3, 113
India 129
Indigenous religions 99, 133
Indigenous technologies 89
Industrial and agricultural revolution 92
Industrial development 88
Infant mortality 44, 84, 91, 93, 94, 112, 118
Inflation 12
Informalization of production 93, 94, 97
Informalization of technology 97
Informal sector 118, 119

Informatics 88, 102
Infrastructure 121
Institute of Advanced Aeronautics and Space Science and Technology 102
Inter-African communications 125
Interdependence 121
Interfutures Project of the Organization for Economic Cooperation and Development 27, 49
International Development Strategy for the 3rd U.N. Development Decade 27, 48
International Institute for Applied Systems Analysis 68
International Institute of Advanced Systems Analysis 15
International Monetary Fund 4, 84, 92, 105, 113
International tariffs 105
Iron and steel industry 61
Irrigated agriculture 56 - 57, 58
  projections for 55, 58
Islam 126

Kalahari 109
Kericho workshop 14, 18, 103
Kimbaguist movements 99
Kugazinza 108
Kulungisa 108

Lagos Plan of Action 7, 14, 27, 123
Lake Tanganyika 109
Land availability 31, 34, 56 - 58
Land tenure 118, 119
Language and culture 108
Legitimization of authority 86
Leontief 49
Lesotho 88, 129
Levers of change 131
Life expectancy 31, 35, 43, 44
Lima Declaration 27, 50
Lingala 101
Literacy 58 - 59
  adult 59
Livestock 115

London School of Economics 118
Loso 108
Luthuli Bay 109

Mabogunje, Prof. Akin 15
McNeill, William H. 12, 13
Madagascar 117
Maize 105
Makerere University 91
Malthusian nightmare 29
Mami Yoko 107
Managers 61
Mandela, Nelson 112, 127
Mandela, Nonkululeko 112
Mandela Plan 121
Manufacturing 49 - 51
Manufacturing Value Added 50, 51
Marginalization of women 97
Marshall Plan 121
Mauritius 42, 43, 44
Marx, Karl 6, 9
Median age 41
Methodology 18 - 23
  interdisciplinary 21
Militarization 95
Military expenditure 121
Millenial movements 99
Millet 105
Mineral energy 62
Mluzi 108
Model for International Relations in Agriculture 55
Mortality 31, 35, 43 - 44
Multilingualism 108
Multiparty systems 134
Music 102
Mutual assistance programme in food aid 122

Nairobi Women's Conference, 2035 89
Namibia 113, 126, 128, 129
Natural gas 63
Natural resources 61 - 72, 88
Networking 23
New African heroes 86

146 BEYOND HUNGER IN AFRICA

New monetary system 85
Nigeria 36, 37, 39, 44, 45
Nkrumah, Kwame 83, 111, 129, 130
Norwegian Ministry of Development Cooperation 16
Nuclear waste disposal 95

Oil 62 – 63, 68, 69
  demand for 68, 69
  producing countries 62
  production 62 – 63
Oil crisis 109
Oil shocks 12, 83
Old-age dependency ratio 40 – 41
Onchocerciasis 116
One-party system 85, 86
Organization of African Unity 4, 122, 126

Pala blight 107
Pan-African Common Market Council 96
Pan-African highway system 87
Pan-African Institute of Advanced Studies 106
Pan Africanism 95, 96, 100, 123, 124, 129, 134
Pan African religious linkages 100 – 101
Panel of Wise Men 14
Parapsychology 107, 134
Parity method 46
Patriots 95
Peaked hydrographs 117
Peasant agriculture 118, 119, 120, 121
Per capita income 33, 35, 91, 93, 103, 112
Persistent-trends scenarios 18
Perverted ethnic questions 106
Pesticide contamination 70
Photovoltaic power 64
Political change 94 – 96
Political kingdom 83, 113
Political legitimacy 95
Political reformation 86, 122 – 125, 133 – 134

Political renewal 122 – 125, 133 – 134
Political stability 113
Pollution 35
Population 8, 27, 29, 31, 33, 34, 36 – 41 91, 93, 103, 112, 121 – 122, 133
  and current perspective, 27, 29, 33 34, 36 – 41
  as a lever of change 133
  growth 93
  growth by country 36 – 40
  growth rate 121 – 123
  in 2057, 33, 34, 91, 103, 112
  J.N. high variant projection 41
  U.N. low variant projection 41
  U.N. medium variant projection 37
Portuguese 100, 101, 108
Power struggles 106
Probability assessment 18, 22
Professional associations 123
Projected per capita 50
Prostitution 97
Psyclimatic diseases 108
PTA 107
PTA currency 103
Pupil-teacher ratio 59
Purchasing power 46

Radioctive contamination 36
Rapid fertility decline 41
Rates of industrialization 93
Reagan, Ronald 127
Recession 93, 105
Reclamation programmes 120
Reconstruction 108, 118 – 122
Recovery 118 – 122
Regional cooperation 95, 113
Regional Food Plan for Africa 55
Regional governments 92
Reilly 69
Rejuvenation 108
Religion 98-100, 125 – 126
Religious diversity 99
Religious renewals 126, 133
Religious tolerance 99
Renewable energy 63 – 66

INDEX 147

Renewal 19, 29, 30
Research 7, 60
Research and Development 60
Research capacity 87
Research topics 131 – 136
Resources 4, 61 – 72, 135
Resource-based ventures 87
Resources for an Uncertain Future 12
Reunion 44
Rift Valley oil 109
Robben Island 112
Ruralization 94

SADCC 85
Sahara 109
Sahel 116
Sanitation 117
Scandinavia 109
School attendance 59
School enrolment ratio 59
Science and technology 96 – 97, 134 – 135
   decline in 95
   demystification of 96
   development of, 1987-2057 96
Science fiction 11
Scientific authors 61
Scientific capacity 60 – 61, 88 – 89, 91
Scientific journals 61
Scientists 60, 61
Second Liberation 85, 86, 88, 89
Second World War 114
Secularization 99
Self image 107
Self reliance 121
Self scrutiny 85
Shabaan Robert Research and Study Centre of Languages and Culture 108
Shaw, Timothy 10
Sierra Leone 44
Silting 117
Single parenthood 97
Social development 28
Social justice 113
Social movements 95

Socialist ideologies 113
Soil erosion 61, 69, 70, 115, 117
Soil fertility 115
Soils 69
Solar energy 64, 88
Sorghum 105
Sorokin 9
Soul-searching 120
South Africa 107, 126, 129, 131, 134
   'Big Push' from 129
   democratic movement in 107
   liberation of 107, 131, 132
   pivotal role of 129
   progress of women in 129
   reconstruction in 129
   repression in 126
South African Economic Community 122
South Africa Regional Economic Cooperation Agreement (SAREC) 85, 87, 88
Space science 91
Spengler 9
Spiritual survival 95
Spontaneous innovations 22
State renewal 133 – 134
Structural adjustments 6, 93
Struggle 92, 113
Subregional organizations 125
Super-conductive discoveries 109, 134
Supervisors 61
Surprises 12, 13
Swahili 100, 108, 125
Swedish Council for Planning and Coordination of Research 15
Swedish International Development Authority 16
Synthetic production 85

Tamed state 96, 133 – 134
Technological capacity 60 – 61, 88 – 89, 91
Technology 8, 60 – 61, 88 – 89, 91
Terms of trade 122
Theatre 102

The New Age 83
Thirty-years drought 106
Three-stage trajectory 19
Total fertility rate 41, 42
Tourist culture 101, 102
Toynbee 9
Traditional culture 89
Traditional symbols 106
Transboundary pollution 72
Trickle-down theory 105
Trouble 19, 28, 29, 30, 104, 105

U.N. Economic Commission for Africa 14, 18
UNESCO 59, 60
U.N. General Assembly's Special Session on the Social and Economic Crisis in Africa, 1986 112, 126
U.N. High Commission for Refugees in Africa 123
U.N. Industrial Development Organization 47, 50
UNITAR 14
U.N. University 14
University 59
Upheavals 90
Uranium 62
Urban crisis 93
Urbanization 44 – 45
Urban waste energy 66
U.S.A. 109
U.S. dollar 84
USSR 109

Voluntary development organizations 87, 123

Wars 90
Water recharge 117
Water shortage 117
Weak commodity prices 83
Welfarist programmes 105
Whiteystan 128
Wind energy 64
World Bank 18, 27, 28, 40, 43, 44, 47, 48, 55, 84, 93
  restructure programmes 6, 84, 93
World Coal Study 62
World Development Report 1984, 47
World Development Report 1986, 47
World Energy Conference Survey 62
World Health Organization 106
World Hunger Programme 15, 16
Worldwatch Institute 4, 112, 116.
Women's emancipation 89, 92, 97 – 98, 119, 129, 133
  in southern Africa 129
Women's organizations 89

Yield 56

Zambia 119
Zimbabwe 119
Zimbabwe Institute of Agricultural Engineering and Environmental Management 120.

Printed by Libri Plureos GmbH in Hamburg, Germany